A World Away

'Peake's widow, painter Maeve Gilmore, tells the story of their life and love simply and unsentimentally . . . but it inevitably makes most impact as the horrific story of a supra-normally gifted man's descent into darkness and silence . . . her tale is unbearably moving in its very reticence. . . . It is a fearful story of the failure of love to penetrate some kinds of suffering, of the extinction of light in an outstandingly rich and inspired mind.' *Financial Times*

'. . . an affecting book . . . an off-beat genius of high, though haunted, imagination and also of remarkable versatility. . . . It was a life with more than its share of burdens and the book pulls no emotional punches.' *The Guardian*

'In tentatively simple prose, Maeve Gilmore re-creates herself and Mervyn loving in their own world. . . . Maeve Gilmore has given us the essence of what Peake was to her alive.' *Times Literary Supplement*

Maeve Gilmore

A WORLD
AWAY
A Memoir of Mervyn Peake

With a preface by Michael Moorcock

Mandarin

A Mandarin Paperback
A WORLD AWAY

First published in Great Britain 1970
by Victor Gollancz Ltd
This edition published 1992
by Mandarin Paperbacks
an imprint of Reed Consumer Books Ltd
Michelin House, 81 Fulham Road, London SW3 6RB
and Auckland, Melbourne, Singapore and Toronto

A CIP catalogue record for this title
is available from the British Library
ISBN 0 7493 1423 0

Printed and bound in Great Britain
by Cox & Wyman Ltd, Reading, Berks

CONTENTS

LIST OF ILLUSTRATIONS

ACKNOWLEDGEMENTS

I am extremely grateful to the following for allowing me to reproduce here letters which they wrote to Mervyn Peake: Sir John Clements, Mr Michael Codron, Mr Graham Greene, Mr Peter Hall, Sir Laurence Olivier, Mr Anthony Quayle and Mr Kenneth Tynan. The B.B.C. have kindly allowed me to reproduce letters written to my husband by Mr David Jones when he was in their employment.

I also gratefully acknowledge the original publishers of poems quoted in this book:

Messrs Bertram Rota for poems from *A Reverie of Bone* ('How foreign to the spirit's early beauty . . .'; 'We are the haunted people'; 'Be proud, slow trees'; 'They had no quiet and smoothed sheets of death . . .'; 'They spire terrific bodies into heaven . . .'; 'Heads float about me . . .'; and '. . . I ponder on sun-lit spires . . .').

Messrs Chatto and Windus for poems from *Shapes and Sounds* ('You walk unaware . . .'; 'The Rhondda Valley'; 'The Cocky Walkers'; 'Coloured Money'; and 'Rather than a little pain . . .').

Messrs Dent for four stanzas from *The Rhyme of the Flying Bomb* ('This isn't no place for the likes of you . . .').

Messrs Eyre and Spottiswoode for two stanzas from a poem in *The Glassblowers* ('With people, so with trees . . .').

'Out of the overlapping leaves . . .' has not previously been published.

PREFACE

My admiration for Mervyn Peake has been one of the few constants in my life. I find it hard to distance myself from the enthusiasm I feel for his work and the affection I felt for him and continue to feel for Maeve Gilmore. This memoir, which was published soon after Mervyn's death in 1968, is still the best and most accurate picture of a remarkable artistic genius and a loveable man whose decline into illness was profoundly terrifying and appallingly unjust. The simplicity and direct-ness of Maeve Gilmore's account of her life with her husband and their children speaks of the rare honesty she and Mervyn shared and which her sons and daughter inherited. No amount of academic interpretation or romantic myth-making can diminish the book's truthfulness.

Since Mervyn's death his reputation and his audience have grown enormously. The public sometimes receives an image of him as a doomed, driven, Byronic artist (perhaps a more suitable personality for the author of the Titus Groan books) when in fact he was a talented, hard-working man of considerable charm and humour, an inspiring, tactful, sensitive teacher, a wonderful friend and parent. As an artist he was constantly developing his range and his techniques. One cannot fail to regret the great loss to the world of all he would have accomplished if he had continued to live in good health.

For the basic facts of Mervyn's life, the most accurate source is John Watney's biography (*Mervyn Peake*, 1976). I was a boy when I first met him in the 1950s, after I had written him an enthusiastic letter, and was invited to tea by Maeve. Their house in Wallington, as Maeve says in this book, was rather like Gormenghast in miniature and my main impression of the interior was of books, pictures and seemingly hundreds of stuffed birds perched on every available surface (Mervyn had bought a job lot some time before). He was already ill and easily tired, but at that time his illness had not been identified as Parkinson's Disease and there was every hope that he would get better. I remember writing, after that first meeting (when I'm certain I outstayed my welcome), that I felt I had for the first time been in the presence of an original genius. I was surprised, too, by the lack of public success Mervyn had received. I began trying to find publishers who would publish or reprint his work. Later this passion was shared by Langdon Jones, who painstakingly put *Titus Alone* back into its original form (the first edition had been somewhat thoughtlessly copy-edited). It was not until Penguin's decision to publish the Titus books that Mervyn's work reached a wide audience. By then Mervyn was too ill to appreciate his success. Since the mid-60s virtually all his work has been republished and his drawings and paintings now change hands for amounts which, had he received a fraction of them at the time, might have made a vast difference to his state of mind.

The person chiefly responsible for Mervyn's increasing recognition is, of course, Maeve Gilmore herself. A gifted painter in her own right she frequently set her own career aside in order to ensure that Mervyn's work received its proper due. As a result it could be argued she gave up the opportunity for consolation as well as personal success, yet there is no hint of self-sacrifice or misdirected piety in this memoir any more than she displays in her own life. A person of enormous courage and dignity, exhibiting the same sense of humour and straightforwardness she reveals in this memoir; a person of great substance, passion and sensibility with a loathing for small-mindedness, meanness and cruelty which, try as she might sometimes, she can never disguise, she has had more than her fair share of misfortune, yet her integrity and love of life has remained fundamentally undamaged. Although I'm sure she would be embarrassed to hear it, *A World Away* is a record of her own love and generosity of soul as much as it is a memoir of Mervyn.

Mervyn was fifty-seven when he died, though his illness made him look considerably older. The illness produced a gradual physical and mental decline and, as his condition worsened, the hope many of us fostered, contrary to the medical evidence, that he would by some miracle get well, began to fade. At the small establishment run by his wife's brother, James Gilmore, Mervyn developed a haemorrhage and died peacefully and, as far as one could tell, happily, for his last months were spent with people who loved and respected him.

I had visited him about a year before. As usual for me the visit had been pleasurable, for although he could remember very little and could rarely finish a sentence, his spirit and his sensibility (as well as his humour) remained. My love for him could not be diminished by the superficial characteristics of his illness. On one level he almost always seemed aware of what had happened to him and at times when strangers patronized him it was possible to see a distinct glint of irony in his eyes. When I heard that he had died, I was filled with rage and then with bitterness. The bitterness, impossible to express still, remains as strong after fifteen years. Mervyn was a man who enjoyed life and gave more to life than anyone I ever knew.

He was a man of great gifts. His vitality was expressed through thousands of drawings and poems and through four novels and two plays. His vision was personal, unselfconscious and to do not with abstractions but with people, of whom he was a wry and sympathetic observer. What gives his Titus books their power and quality is not so much their fantastic elements as their characters—the Earl and Countess of Groan, Flay and Swelter, Steerpike, Fuchsia Groan, Irma Prunesquallor and Doctor Prunesquallor, the mad twins Cora and Clarice, Barquentine and a hundred others—who have bizarre names, certainly, but are as alive and credible as Dickens's characters. Like Dickens, Peake had the gusto, the energy, the invention, the powers of observation, the language, the skill to direct his flood of original invention.

One of Peake's most remarkable qualities was his crafts-manship, his control over the creations of his unique imagination. This control was observable in everything he drew and wrote. He is generally considered the finest illustrator of his day, although the commissions he received were comparatively few—*The Rime of the Ancient Mariner, Treasure Island, Alice in Wonderland, Grimm's Household Tales, The Hunting of the Snark* and a handful of others—and not always as well-paid as they should have been. Dozens of drawings could be mentioned: his portraits of children, his drawings of Belsen inmates, his sketches of Sark, Spain and all the other places he lived in or visited. His talent was unmarred by any hint of the morbid neurosis frequently identified with artists of such intensity; he had no political axes to grind, no messianic notions, no manifestoes to justify or rationalize his particular view of the world. Such things amused him and were often his subject-matter (the emphasis in the Titus books, for instance, on ritual and the quest for power). He was concerned with the business of living, astonished by earnest discussions on the Nature of Art and Life, reduced to laughter by the antics of bureaucrats and politicians and, as his old friend the Rev. A. C. Bridge told those who attended, would have been acutely embarrassed by his own Memorial Service which was held at St James's Church, Piccadilly, on 6 December 1968.

Mervyn had a fine eye for irony. His work could often be

sardonic, but there was no malice in him; merely a considerable sympathy for the individual, particularly the underdog. His amusement at fixed ideologies was neither innocent nor naive, but it was frequently disbelieving. Perhaps it was his refusal to rationalize and explain his work that made it hard for critics to 'place' him and why his work made many, whose attitudes were conventionally moulded, uncomfortable or antagonistic, why, as a consequence, a large public took so long to 'find' him.

Mervyn would have been particularly amused to hear himself called a seminal figure, yet there is no doubt he influenced and continues to influence many new writers, especially in subject-matter and technique. He certainly had considerable influence on what I think is my own best work. His spirit lives on in those he has inspired, in his remarkable family (Maeve now has ten grandchildren) and, of course, in his own work, which so accurately reflects his attitude to the world:

> To live at all is miracle enough,
> The doom of nations is another thing.
> Here is my hammering blood-pulse is my proof.
>
> Let every painter paint and poet sing
> And all the sons of music ply their trade;
> Machines are weaker than a beetle's wing.
>
> Swung out of sunlight into cosmic shade,
> Come what come may the imagination's heart
> Is constellation high and can't be weighed.
>
> Nor greed nor fear can tear our faith apart
> When every heart-beat hammers out the proof
> That life itself is miracle enough.

(*The Glassblowers*, 1950)

In one of his rare published statements about work (*Drawings of Mervyn Peake*, 1949) he said: 'After all, there are no rules. With the wealth, skill, daring, vision of many centuries at one's back, yet one is ultimately quite alone. For it is one's ambition to create one's *own* world in a style germane to its substance, and to people it with its native forms and denizens that never were before, yet have their roots in one's experience. As the earth was thrown from the sun, so from the earth the artist must fling out into space, complete from pole to pole, his own world which, whatsoever form it takes, is the colour of the globe it flew from, as the world itself is coloured by the sun.'

Mervyn Peake succeeded splendidly in creating his own world—a richly populated world—and he left it for us to enjoy.

Since this memoir was first published Mervyn's work has appeared all over the world and film rights have been bought for *Gormenghast*. His main fiction has never been long out of print. Books which he illustrated have been republished because there is now a large audience for his drawings. He is 'collected' (copies of first editions, particularly of illustrated books, sometimes selling for more than the advance he originally received) and he is 'taught'. There is a Mervyn Peake Society, publishing a regular journal, and he is the subject of academic theses. His reputation and his audience is assured; he is recognized as one of the important figures in post-war English literature. I suppose it is unrealistic to wish that some of this recognition had come a little earlier (if only in the form of somewhat larger advances) and to continue to regret the fact that Mervyn never really understood what his work meant to the generations who followed him; he so thoroughly deserved the rewards of his own generosity.

A World Away is a unique book, capturing experience and intensity of feeling without a note of false sentiment or bathos.

Maeve Gilmore is no more capable of self-consciousness in her writing than was her husband. It is, as I've said, a book of remarkable truthfulness. It remains one of the most moving books I have ever read. It will endure, in its own right, for as long as the work of that great artist whose humanity it so effortlessly celebrates.

Michael Moorcock
Fulham Road
London
May 1983

Into the sculpture room he came, quick and sudden and dark, and when he left the room they said, 'That's Mervyn Peake; he's dying of consumption.' For me, at seventeen, someone dying of consumption (even though he was not) had a terrible romance about it.

He returned a few minutes later to the sculpture room, went to the tin trunk where the damp clay was kept, scooped out a handful of it, then went to work on it. In a very short space of time, a vigorous figure emerged from the hitherto shapeless clay; it had nothing to do with the prosaic pose of the model, or the even more prosaic efforts of the students. It had grown out of a native exuberance, and it was the first time I had seen such vitality manifest itself.

During the break, this volatile, dark man came over to where I stood, palpitating, in front of my own clay. He asked me to meet him that evening when the classes were over—perhaps to go to a park for a walk. Out of my appalling shyness I said that I never went for walks, and I didn't like parks. Perhaps such a bald answer should have ended everything before it began, but I did manage to ask, 'What do you paint?' and the answer, 'I'd paint a dust-bin if I thought it beautiful,' was by far the strangest thing I had ever heard, especially coming from the most romantic looking man I had ever seen, that I managed to accept an invitation to tea, which followed this startling dust-bin manifesto.

It had been my first day at an art school, September 1936. I was a convent-reared girl, with a built-in nervousness. It took me an half-hour to enter the school, the cloak-rooms, and eventually the class. It was an experience that I had never before encountered, and the inhibitions with which I had commenced adolescence were too intense to accept without questioning the world of easy banter, in which everyone seemed to know what they were doing and saying. Perhaps no one knew but when one is unsure everyone else seems to be perfectly at ease.

He left the sculpture room, leaving behind him the clay figure he had modelled. The rest of the day for me seemed as long as a climb up Everest.

It did end though, and I went down the stairs to the hall of the school, feeling now as though I was descending Everest, such trepidation and fright did I feel at entering an unknown world. The experience of climbing Everest had changed the world from which I had come. It could no longer be the same—would one's feet ever touch the ground again?

He was waiting in the hall, in the longest, shabbiest, darkest-grey mackintosh that I had ever seen. He looked like a young handsome gypsy, or a young tramp, slim and dark, with the deep-set eyes, and heavy eyelids that were so very striking, and the deep furrows down his cheeks—too deep for so young a man.

     ★   ★   ★

There were still trams at that time, and we went upstairs in one. Along Vauxhall Bridge Road it went, and rattled loud enough to make conversation very difficult, like talking or listening through chain mail. That was good for me, as all thoughts, or rather all intelligent thoughts, had completely vanished, and I could think of nothing to say of my own volition, and nothing to answer.

Eventually, we arrived at a Lyons Corner House, and went upstairs to a balcony where one could see the gypsy ladies' band downstairs. In memory they almost seem like caricatures, but the music was being played with electrifying gusto. It was in this Corner House that for us both love began to the strains of 'The Desert song'. What a desert, what a song.

I was put back on a tram: it couldn't have been the end of an evening, only the beginning of living. I arrived home somehow, and to me the whole world was vibrating. I couldn't imagine a world without Peake—as I thought of him. It was some time before I could use his first name to myself or to anyone else. It was private, and it hurt.

At the time when I first saw Mervyn, and first met him, I had no previous knowledge of him, although he had had exhibitions in a Soho gallery with a group of painters who called themselves the 'Twenties Group', mainly his fellow students from the Royal Academy Schools; and all, as the name implies, in their twenties. Looking through old catalogues which have survived the years, the prices seem very modest, usually between five and fifteen guineas.

Peake was not a student in the sculpture room, but he was teaching—life-drawing. A different part of life. I longed to see him again. He phoned to ask me to go to see him in the place where he lived and worked, and painted. I was given directions. They seemed remote, but as directions always seemed remote to me I knew that I should have to have them transcribed by someone who read maps. A warehouse just over Battersea Bridge, and past a bus station depot. I had seen for years, across the river, a huge signpost which read 'Thousands of tons wasted daily'. I had seen it, and it had meant nothing—just one of those things, like disease, and old age, which we know about but have no inkling of, because it has not touched one personally. 'Thousands of tons wasted daily' was the slogan which pulled one into life.

My first visit was very circumspect. I gave the directions to Penfold, my mother's chauffeur—'Hester Road', just across Battersea Bridge, past the bus station.

Oh, how I love the memory of that place. The incongruousness of it, and my particular form of arrival never struck me as strange. How could it? When one is in a trance, reality seems the strange thing.

I knocked at a battered door, and I heard steps descending. The door opened. Penfold stayed outside, and I never gave another thought to him. He must have been in an alien world himself more so even than me, but he waited patiently outside for several hours, until I stepped down the stairs, another girl in another clime, never to return to what I had thought I knew.

There was a flight of stairs leading directly from the door—the steps were painted a crude chrome yellow, and the top of the banisters vermilion. At the top of the stairs there was a succession of rooms. I had never seen anything like them. They were not furnished. They were simply alive. Paintings and drawings everywhere. Dark patches on the walls, which I presume must have been patches of damp, but faces and landscapes had been woven into them, so that what should have been detrimental was turned into a world of angels and monsters.

A hissing of an ancient gasfire welcomed one, an old chaise-longue in front of it; and in the corners of each of the rooms, and not in corners, were collections of more empty and half-empty milk bottles than I had ever seen. The most beautiful and the most romantic place I had been to.

I can remember nothing of that first visit, except that I knew that I must and would return there.

*   *   *

After this first visit, I was able to find my own way, down Hester Road, past the bus-drivers and the conductors. I hated going past them, because of the jokes and the whistles. But once in those rooms, I entered a new world. Silent, except for the intermittent, or perhaps regular, vulgar noises of the ancient gasfire, which was also inefficient as a means of

Mervyn Peake, 1946

Mervyn Peake,
1935

The family,
Sark, 1949

heating. Such beautiful rooms, bare of comfort. Mervyn, as I was beginning to be able to call him, did drawings and paintings of me: a head turning; a body standing; a half head; an eye; a mouth; a hand; half-draped; half-nude; draped or nude; lying; sitting; asleep; awake; laughing; crying; singing; sulking; pencil; pen; oil; chalk; and over-all the nostalgic smell of turpentine.

And afterwards, toasted crumpets by the fire, and indifferent tea.

The stairway to the attic—the stairway to Fuchsia's attic in *Titus Groan*—was larger than life, though what could be larger than life as it was lived in those days?

Sitting by the fire, in this quiet enchanted world, there would sometimes and suddenly be the sound of thuds, and unexpected sound overhead. This island was after all an island surrounded by water, by the Thames. Warehouses on rivers are the refuges of large river rats. Large river rats can jump dexterously, and can pilfer ingeniously; paper and canvas could be quite a pleasant diet. Romance survived on the sound, and only once the sight of these huge and frightening river inhabitants disturbed us.

Once in the candlelight, in front of the black gas monster, the floorboards of the room seemed to move very gently, undulating with the lazy ease of a hammock. It wasn't the candlelight which was playing tricks, because there was also an accompaniment of sound, the sound of the trumpeting of an elephant. The sound and the movement seemed like a minor earth tremor. The sound of an elephant trumpeting was the sound of an elephant trumpeting, and the sight of the floorboards moving was the heaving of the elephant moving underneath. It was being housed for the night in the warehouse below on its way to dance and sing in a travelling circus.

★   ★   ★

These days were translucent—with light, if love is light, or light is love. They were days of love, but of discovery also. To see everything in a new way. Everything was new. Battersea Bridge, the Embankment, have never been more beautiful. Walking along by the river at dusk and going into 'The Blue Cockatoo', which has now disappeared, for some tea by candlelight. Talking of the future, of the present, of painting, of poetry, jokes. Watching, and being watched, for certainly then Mervyn was an unusual sight. His hair was long and very dark, and he wore bright red waistcoats, orange velvet ties, and occasionally odd socks: one red, one white, not to be looked at, but because he was even then absent-minded. He had a black cloak, with a red lining. People always seemed to stare, at what today would pass unnoticed. But apart from being looked at himself, Mervyn looked and taught me to look, to see people and incidents, objects, and to store up knowledge. People were the raw material for many of his illustrations. Sometimes he would stop a stranger in the street—it could be a tramp, it could be a girl, or a spiv—and ask him to pose, perhaps on the spot, a quick drawing (sometimes on the inside of a cigarette carton, if he had no sketch-book with him), and sometimes to go to his studio, when he would do drawings or paintings of him.

When I was still a somewhat young bride, the girls he stopped always seemed to have good 'bone structure', which eased the small green seed of jealousy, and later on 'bone structure' became one of those jokes enjoyed only between ourselves.

Apart from this, the drawings made of an old tramp asleep in Trafalgar Square were used for the Baker in *Hunting of the Snark*, which was one of the first books he illustrated. I remember seeing a man coming out of Hatchards in Piccadilly with a copy under his arm, and I walked up to him and said, 'My husband did those drawings.' I was frozen by a look. I had invaded a private universe, and I decided that it were better to remain silent, always.

*   *   *

For Mervyn, going down into the underground was not a straightforward, upright, and still journey down an escalator, but a sliding descent down the rail. I could never summon up courage to follow, so that sometimes he would reach the bottom, go up the other escalator, and pass me by once more at, it seemed, even greater speed, in time to take my hand as I staidly tripped off the bottom step.

We often went to Lyons for meals, and I suppose we were neither of us the most regular looking customers: Mervyn, I know, was unique, dark and majestic. How can I say what I was? I think: pale and blonde and a good foil for such a dark one. Mervyn sometimes ordered stewed camel. It probably wasn't very funny, and the waitresses obviously thought not. They raised their eyebrows, and tapped their pencil on their pad, until the conventions were observed, and they were back in the world of brunch or eggs and chips, which they understood.

In the first years we found Lyons shops a kind of home. Once we met James Stephens, the Irish poet, like a little leprechaun, curly haired and lively, witty and from a world of fairies, and we all went in to the Lyons in Leicester Square. This was just after we were married, and he wrote a little poem for me on a scrap of paper which I still have.

For all Young Brides

When a son you shall desire
Pray to water, and to fire.

But when you would have a daughter
Pray to fire and then to water.

Then he did a strange little drawing which he called 'Portrait of many Mervyn Peakes by his friend James Stephens. Given at this Court at Lyons Dive 1938'.

* * *

Before our love went too far, I was sent away. For some strange and now quite forgotten reason I wished to learn German. So I went to a castle (probably a minor one) on the Rhine. The father, killed in the First World War, and the mother, a Baronin, picking up bits of silver paper on the spike of her walking-stick for munitions for the next war. Oh, how stupid, how ignorant one was as a girl. The terrible demonstrations for Hitler that I saw, but didn't understand, thinking only of love. The Nazi salutes, which one unthinkingly returned, as though it were a charade. The joke which was beyond one. I saw Hitler once at a parade in Nuremberg, and I saw Hess, and my mind had only one thought. Love.

My first letter from Mervyn in Germany was a drawing, a group of girls all walking with their feet fixed on back to front; and the caption: 'Is this how they walk?' Where has the drawing gone? Lost, anyway.

But love was not lost. It survived a year, and we met again as though only a flutter of an eyelid had passed.

* * *

I went down to see Mervyn's parents in Wallington, Surrey. I felt frightened to meet them. I couldn't imagine him having parents. I couldn't imagine him coming from anywhere but from himself, and I didn't want to see him in any kind of environment but his own.

I was wrong. His father was kind and slow of speech, searching always for the apposite word, and always finding it, however long it took. His mother was small, dark, lively, and

Mervyn's dark looks were from Wales, his mother's native land.

His father was now a general practitioner, having returned from China. The change of environment must have been like the difference between space travel and under-sea diving.

The house was large, Victorian and Gothic, and much of its interior had reminders of the life which had been left behind: rice bowls and dragons, Chinese carpets, ornate brass ornaments. Later, as I learned to know them better, many of the horrifying experiences they had undergone during the Boxer Rising, and the violence they received as 'white devils', came to light, and I felt a pride in their achievements, which now have been erased in Communist China, but which must have taken them so very much courage and foresight.

Mervyn's father drew delicate little drawings, and his mother sang and played the piano, and from these must have sprung his own gifts. I think they themselves must have often wondered how such a gifted son had arrived through them. They were rather shocked by his first exhibition of line drawings, which had a sensuousness not to be expected from the son of a medical missionary.

I know that his father had seen very dreadful and appalling sights during the Rebellion, and his own work amongst people who were suspicious of the foreign devil was carried on under conditions which would appal and deter the surgeons of today. It was a long time before he was accepted in Tientsin, where he wished to build a hospital, and the occasion which made it possible is, or must be, medically bizarre. The local mandarin had a son who was blind, and he was brought to Dr Peake, after a great deal of courteous and non-committal exchange of pleasantries.

On examination, he was found to have cataract in both eyes. It must have been almost impossible to explain in the most difficult language of Mandarin China the effect that an operation on the eyes might have. Somehow there was a mutual understanding, and it was decided that an operation would be acceptable, but only if it were performed in public with the father and his entourage watching.

I do not know the details, as there is no one living who can substantiate them. All I know is that Mervyn's father was a man of courage. If he had failed, his life—or perhaps less so, his reputation—was at stake.

The operation was duly performed, and it had in some way been conveyed to the father that there would be no immediate result. It would take time before the bandages were removed from the eyes, and the result would be slow in manifesting itself.

After a length of time, perhaps two weeks, the bandages were removed for the first time, and an object held in front of the eyes. Before an audience of father and courtiers, there was a flicker of sight.

This happened over another period of time, and the young man saw. The foreign devil had expunged himself and the mandarin gave financial help to the building of a hospital.

A sad aftermath of this successful operation was the sight of a column of very poor blind Chinese, one behind the other, each holding the pigtail of the one in front, making their way to the surgery and falling down on their knees, praying for sight, to the man they could neither see nor understand. Impossible to explain in a distant language that theirs was blindness, and congenital. How could they understand? They left the way they had arrived, with their only security the pigtail of their blind friend or enemy in front of them, and only thinking that they were sinful and unworthy of the miracle that had been worked on the mandarin's son.

* * *

The digression to Mervyn's parents is not a digression. His

childhood was unusual, and I can see in his work so much that sprang from the surroundings that enveloped him, although to everyone in this particular world, which retained so much a flavour of England, but surrounded by China, it must have seemed quite mundane.

A strange childhood. Such a mixture of English nonconformity, and almost bourgeois convention. Congregational hymns, tea-parties, a straight-laced upbringing, and outside surrounded by dragons and carvings of ancient imagination and disastrous beauty.

He rode on a mule to Tientsin Grammar School, where he received the most English of educations. His most vivid recollection seems to be of the raw red elbows of the spinster teacher who ran the school, although for some reason his parents lived in the Russian compound. So many things which are called 'Gothic' in his *Titus Groan* trilogy must spring from the fantasies which presented themselves to him, years later, from his childhood in China.

One day, on his mule, he stretched out his hand to stroke a camel. They are vicious creatures and not used to love. He could hear for ever after the livid meeting of the camel's jaws, as they opened and closed on what should have been his hand. A coolie, in a quick gesture, had pulled Mervyn's hand away, and he was left trembling, silent, and tearful, but with a right hand intact.

That camel made an appearance, perhaps thirty-five years later, in *Titus Alone*. It was a vile camel.

On his way to school he passed the tragic huts outside the compound, where the poorest lived, and the stray dogs, scrawny with hunger, sniffed and dug and scratched for what little sustenance they could find.

Mervyn was perhaps seven years old. Did he understand? And where did he store these sights, this knowledge, for the compound to make its way into *Titus Groan*, thirty years later, as the habitation of the mud-dwellers, who carved for their love, and their life, and the dreadful lean dogs, stalking their way through the dwellings?

He returned to England at the age of eleven with his parents and his brother. They came via the Trans-Siberian Railway. A few adolescent memories recurred to him. His brother, getting off the train, whilst it was being refuelled, in mid-Siberia, and the slow advance of the train in this desolate grey ice-pack. As it mounted speed, the small speck of humanity being left behind for the wolves. The mother, calling and calling for her child, who ran, faster than was thought possible, and being pulled by his father as though his arms would be torn to shreds, on to the high steps of the train—and the small younger brother, agog with excitement and trepidation. In his excitement, throwing out shoes, socks, gloves, but in such a situation, who cares what is expended! The small or larger boy was saved from the wolves, and life lay ahead, unexpected and unforearmed.

The carvings were everywhere, buildings were not functional but full of fantasy. How could it not have influenced a mind which from somewhere had a vision that finally betrayed it by its richness?

*   *   *

The visit to Wallington in Surrey, to meet Mervyn's parents, seemed to bring closer an event which now had an inevitability about it. Neither of us could imagine a life ahead which was not shared with the other.

Formalities seemed necessary, although we would both have liked to marry in some remote, isolated church, close to the sea, or dark and candlelit. But what one wants is not necessarily what is decided upon.

My parents met Mervyn. He had many things which were

not in his favour. Certainly, no one in the family had seen anyone quite like him before—with his dark, long hair, his deep-sunken eyes, shielded by black eyelashes, his red waistcoats, his purple socks, his orange velvet tie, all this and his lack of money. Perhaps most of all, the creed in which he had spent his childhood. Nonconformity. But religious nonconformity. His own life was nonconformist in ideas, his ideas were nonconformist in his life.

Somehow the divergencies had to be met. Divergencies are always met by the charitable. The practising Christians with their creeds, with their small partitions and lack of charity are the ones who win outwardly.

> How foreign to the spirit's early beauty
> And to the amoral integrity of the mind
> And to all those whose reserve of living is lovely
> Are the tired Creeds that can be so unkind.
>
> There is brotherhood among the kindly,
> Closer and defter and more integral
> Than any brotherhood of aisle or coven
> For love rang out before the chapel bell.
>
> There is no intolerance and no bitterness
> As between sects where the full-hearted are
> And to pray for the non-natural and to have pity
> On those of alien faith whose eyes are clear
>
> Is to be insolent, is to be ignorant,
> Is to deny the god-head—is to withhold
> The focal Christ of love; is to renounce
> The only selfless language in the world.

Jesus—where are you?
That is me speaking, after Mervyn. It seems it is not

possible to live by love alone. Dogma—laws of the church, laws of man—are essential to respectability.

I loved my mother very much. Mervyn loved me, and I loved Mervyn. No one wants to hurt anyone they love. I would have lived with Mervyn without any of the formalities, although I was devout to a degree of intensity.

I still don't want to hurt—but why is it that they hurt me? because my creed has changed; and I hurt them. Mervyn can no longer be hurt or hurt, although he was the gentlest man alive—a gentleness that came from his father who, having seen the cruelties of human beings, had retained an innocence that was touching and impossible to understand.

*   *   *

We were married very conventionally in St James's, Spanish Place. All the concessions came from the other side. From people who had spent their lives with a creed that had little to do with popery, who did not understand the dogma and the ritual but who were willing to concede on behalf of a son who loved a being so different as to be almost from another planet.

Theirs was the generous spirit.

*   *   *

So life began.

Could one possibly know what life was? How could one know what love was, before living it? How could one know what life was before loving it?

We lived in a flat overlooking Battersea Park, from December 1937. It didn't matter to me where we lived, and such mundane things as eating or meeting people or earning a living seemed utterly extraneous, vulgar and not germane to us. The gentle veil of love surrounded us—oh, why do we wake?

About this time, there was a great deal of abuse against a piece of sculpture by Jacob Epstein, called Adam. Strange that people no longer become incensed by painting or sculpture in the way that they used to. Mervyn wrote a poem, called 'Epstein's Adam', and sent it to *Picture Post*, where it was given quite a bit of space. It was written as a protest at protest. A few days later Epstein wrote to ask Mervyn to come to see him. We both went to tea in a mansion of a house in Hyde Park Gardens. There was sculpture everywhere. It was a moving manifestation of a man obsessed. We had tea at a huge table presided over by his first wife, an over-life-size woman, with deep red hair. I always think of her as Gertrude in *Titus Groan*—whether she was some kind of inspiration for her (although that sounds an archaic word) I have no idea.

Apart from the abundance of work everywhere, the only thing I remember is a detailed and absorbing description by his son, a small intelligent boy, of the refuelling of aeroplanes in the air, a subject about which neither Mervyn nor I was knowledgeable.

I knew nothing of cooking, nothing of cleaning; it seems on looking back that I simply knew nothing of anything. I had very little conversation; I had hardly heard of ideas as ideas. I can think of no one more boring. When we went out to meet people, if I was addressed personally, I simply went red, stuttered, and burst into tears. One of the first occasions this happened was when we went into a group of what I presume were intellectuals, and I was asked point-blank what I thought of the new Peter Jones building. Quite honestly, I had never thought it was a subject to be thought about. In the deathly silence which awaited my answer, and the white blankness which enveloped me, there was nothing to say, except; 'I think . . . it's negative', and then a burst of tears, and the embarrassment which followed such anti-social behaviour took us off home before our time.

The main source of income then was still the teaching—
life-drawing twice a week at the Westminster School of Art
where we had met, and commissions by the now defunct
London Mercury (which was published monthly, and brought a
small addition to our budget) to do drawings of already
famous authors, artists, actors and actresses.

There was never any organized time for working—how
could there be? An idea for a poem would grow as suddenly as
the flight of a meteor. It might be jotted down quickly on the
inside of a cigarette carton, to be worked on later. In the
middle of the night words were eased into birth, to grow into a
poem, the next day and following days or weeks, difficult as
life itself.

Twice a week teaching, and the remaining five days filled
with creative activity so rich and varied that one wonders how
one man could survive such an onslaught on his eyes, ears, and
brain.

*   *   *

It was in 1938 that the first exhibition of drawings of
Mervyn's had been arranged. An exhibition of line drawings
at a gallery called The Calmann Gallery just off St James's. It
seemed to presage hope.

Hitler marched into, oh God, was it Czechoslovakia? or was
it Vienna? on the day of the private view. So much does
history impinge on our individual lives. A desperate air. As
desperate as today. I remember standing on the balcony
overlooking Battersea Park the night before the exhibition
opened, and the dreadful feeling of foreboding. Not because
for the first time in his life Mervyn was putting himself in view
of a public who might be antagonistic or receptive, but
because of a malaise—a political tremor which shook
everyone; for even then it was hard to remain aloof, although
the world has shrunk further since those days.

The first taste of a personal success, even a minor one, was damaged by outside events, which were the beginning of total world damage.

The sale of the first drawing was to me like selling my body. It was a drawing of me, which seemed to be intimate, and entirely belonging to us, as was the love we generated. Private and alone. It seemed inconceivable that a drawing, made alone and imperatively, should go into a house of strangers, hang on their walls, and be looked at, liked or disliked, spoken of by people we didn't know or care about. I wept once more at this concession to the philistine world. Gradually one's tears dry, and the cliché that time heals begins to rear its practical head.

Eddie Marsh, who collected pictures like butterflies, bought a drawing, and later a very large oil painting. He asked us both to come to see him, in one of the Inns of Court. Even though my house has an infinity of pictures, I have never seen anything quite like his! Pictures three or four deep wherever one looked. I think he was the first example of a really erudite man that I had ever met. Mervyn remained solely himself in whatever company he kept, whilst I was intimidated and frightened by such a superior brain.

★   ★   ★

The exhibition was financially a moderate success. There had been reviews. The first taste. Now I can read, on Mervyn's behalf, the good, the bad, the indifferent with a cauterized mind and still survive the day.

★   ★   ★

Just before we were married, Mervyn took me down to see Walter de la Mare in Buckinghamshire. Our meeting came about through a poem which Mervyn had written to me, and which Walter de la Mare wished to include in an anthology called *Love* which he was editing.

How can I say that the poem was not one which brought pride and love to me?

> You walk unaware
> Of the slender gazelle
> That moves as you move
> And is one with the limbs
> That you have.
>
> You live unaware
> Of the faint, the unearthly
> Echo of hooves
> That throughout your white streams
> Of clear clay that I love
>
> Are in flight as you turn
> As you stand, as you move,
> As you sleep, for the slender
> Gazelle never rests
> In your ivory groove.

He had been almost a myth for so long, since my school days and the learning of 'The Traveller', that I couldn't believe he existed, and he was the first famous person that I ever met.

We went by train to Penn, then walked to his house from the station. I was sick from apprehension on the walk to his house, but little I knew how unnecessary that was, for the man was gentle and fanciful, able to make the most diffident of guests at home in his house. He was small, and bright eyed. His wife also had the gift of putting at ease anyone who seemed uneasy.

We had tea at a candlelit table, and the talk ranged from

subject to subject—ghosts, love, fancy, stories—and as de la Mare wrote a little later in a letter which seems apposite:

> One sips at a subject, and then passes on to flower No. 2, and so forth, does show up the peculiar evanescence of one's thoughts and fancies. These can be so infernally rapid; and yet I'm rather inclined to think that mine are like one of those charming little toys of my childhood when you peeped at a succession of the same figure in different attitudes etc.—whirled him round and he became alive. In quite other words, don't you think one finds oneself dishing out the same little obsessions over and over again. I simply cannot resist anything in the nature of apparitional.

That is almost how the conversation went. After tea, we went into the drawing-room, where de la Mare showed us his collection of miniature books. Beautifully made and perfect. It was some years later that I read a book of his, *Memoirs of a Midget*, and recollected this unusual and strangely personal set of tiny books.

There was a dream-like quality over the whole of that first meeting, and all the subsequent times. There was nothing to be frightened of in such a dulcet man.

★   ★   ★

The first commission for an illustrated book of Nursery Rhymes came at about this time. It was called *Ride a Cock-Horse* and had fourteen illustrations. It was quite easily the most beautifully produced of the books that Mervyn illustrated. The war had started, but the paper shortage and the many restrictions connected with publishing hadn't yet begun to make their indelible and ugly mark on wartime books.

Walter de la Mare wrote to say:

I have been engrossed in Nursery Rhyme pictures again and again. Fantasy and the grotesque, indeed; a rare layer of the imagination, and a touch now and then, and more than a touch of the genuinely sinister. But, as I think, not a trace of the morbid—that very convenient word. How many nurseries you may have appalled is another matter. How many scandalized parents may have written to you, possibly enclosing doctor's and neurologist's bills, you will probably not disclose. Anyhow, most other illustrated books for children look just silly by comparison.

*   *   *

In 1938 we moved from Battersea to two floors of a house in Portsdown Road in Maida Vale. A very short walk to the canal, and a district which seemed rather dingy. The rooms we had were the precursors of the succession of houses and flats in which we lived afterwards. They were nearly always large, very high-ceilinged, and usually in need of decoration, except that books and pictures in profusion were always our major decorative effort. Often murals on the walls, and doors decorated like rococo cathedrals.

In a flat downstairs to which we were invited the owners had a passion for red. Both had dyed red hair, but on being shown into their rooms we were smothered and felt claustrophobic with vermilion—walls, carpets, ceiling, chairs, sofas, all in more tones and shades of red than could be imagined. We wondered what their politics were! But I don't think fanatical manifestoes made their way out of all this decorative fantasia. They just loved red.

In our own home we had a tortoise who appropriated the fire with our two cats: a black one called Chakka, the Black Napoleon, and a white one called Moby Dick. The tortoise roamed round the room gently and quietly, poking its little

Mervyn Peake in Soho whilst on leave, 1944

The author, 1937

raddled head out of its shell with the serenity of a cave-bound hermit, and eating up what greens there were. I found it strange that one could even grow to have a little affection for such an unknown quantity which housed itself in a shell.

Early in 1939 Mervyn had his second exhibition of paintings and drawings, at the Leicester Galleries; and I had my first exhibition at the Wertheim Galleries. There was a radio programme called 'In Town To-night', and we were asked to be on it, on the strength of our having concurrent exhibitions.

Quite naturally, we were in the usual state of inadequate finances, and we were told that we would each receive £3, which seemed a fortune in minuscule. We had one rehearsal, and on the evening went up to Broadcasting House, as two of the interesting people 'In Town To-night'! One of the others was Lilli Palmer, and her sister, and we all sat outside the studio, feeling vastly uninteresting.

It was far less arduous than we imagined, and we left the studio £6 the richer, and made our way straight to the Café Royal. Instead of the usual coffee, sitting on red plush seats at marble tables, we went beyond the barrier to the tables laid for eating. The £6 receded, as the meal proceeded, and there was very little left of the riches received that evening.

Sometimes we had a group of people in to do drawings from a model, and then we would have coffee and talk, or dance after drawing. It seems like a pre-historic way of spending an evening now, but then there was the dreadful malaise of an imminent war that diversions, of work or play, could not eliminate.

We had passed 'Peace in our Time', in which people believed because they so wished for it—although how could we have believed it, with so much menace, so much flavour of despair or inevitability surrounding us all?

Nevertheless, individuals still made their plans, had their hopes and aspirations.

My mother lent us a car to go to Stratford-on-Avon for a few days, in the beginning of September 1939. England looked invitingly beautiful—we were afraid for its vulnerability, aware of how easily the beauty could be damaged. We went to see *As You Like It* at the Stratford Memorial Theatre, and I remember an old man sitting in front of us, who so entered into the excitement of the fight between the wrestlers on stage that he stood up and encouraged his chosen one in a hoarse and excitable voice, flinging his arms around menacingly at the opponent, and shouting belligerently as though he were truly in a wrestling ring.

Such anti-social behaviour could not be allowed to last long, and he was asked by the manager to remove himself. We thought it was a marvellous tribute to the actors that he had so entered into the spirit of the play.

It was a time when one could be lost for a short while in dreams, but there was always the awakening to reality, knowing that life as we were living it then could not, would not, ever be the same again. Outside events would engulf everyone.

We were in Chipping Campden. The Cotswolds hurt us by their opulence; and Mervyn wrote this poem:

> We are the haunted people.
> We, who guess blindly at the seed
> That flowers
> Into the crimson caption,
> Hazarding
> The birth of that inflamed
> Portentous placard that will lose its flavour
> Within the hour,
> The while the dark deeds move that gave the words
> A bastard birth
> And hour by hour

Bursts a new gentian flower
Of bitter savour
We have no power . . . no power . . .
We are the haunted people,
We . . .
The last loose tassellated fringe that flies
Into the cold of aeons from a dark
Dynastic gown.

★   ★   ★

We were staying in a hotel in the square, and on the
morning of 3 September 1939, we heard the bell of a
town-crier ringing with an urgency that could only presage
one thing. The tricorne hat and the long cape-coat, the bell,
and the parchment had something about them of permanence,
and the announcement of war seemed less dreadful, couched
in the archaic language and setting of what seemed to be an
England of ancient custom.

Just as the town-crier finished calling out the news which
everyone was hearing in so many different ways and en-
vironments all over England, an almost apocalyptical figure,
a man, appeared from one side of the square on a white horse
and rode to the other side, disappearing as suddenly as he
came, so that one hardly knew if it were a vision or not. He
remained as a symbol always, through the war years to come.

What did one feel at that time? A dreadful fear of the
unknown. But even in the time of such overwhelming fear,
our own personal lives cannot but have importance to us, and
hearing the announcement of war with the knowledge that we
were expecting our first child could only cast gloom on an
event which in itself is so mysterious.

We left Gloucestershire and returned to London. To the flat
in Maida Vale. Everything had a strangeness: the atmosphere

was uncertain, yet people still laughed and quarrelled, made love, were apprehensive, knew nothing, wished to do something positive, loved England, and more and more floundered in a negative abyss. Mervyn volunteered to fit gas masks, and was accepted; for the world, or England at war, was still uncertain, and until he was called up this seemed the only occupation for which he was suited.

These months from September onwards had an unreality about them that is like the unreality one feels before an operation—or before the birth of a child—the ominousness that precedes a violent change, so that one is never the same again.

The first Christmas of the war came, and the expected violence was non-existent, at least as we had visualized it over England, in England. We were still in Maida Vale. Our red friends downstairs blacked out, our friends upstairs with a fencing studio were gone; and we were left with our huge windows, criss-crossed with tape, hung with black draperies.

We wished to make Christmas memorable in a way to do with peace, as though life was as it had always been. Our finances were not outstandingly affluent—in fact, were as they had always been, a little strained—but we decided to buy as many packets of cigarettes as could stand the strain, and then for Mervyn to go with them to the Arches, and give a packet, to whomsoever he saw, as a minute gesture of Christmas. The Arches were beneath Waterloo Bridge where the derelict and the homeless congregated, the sordid and the lonely.

About midnight on Christmas morning he returned, empty of cigarettes, but with a young Welsh coal-miner whom he had found in the Arches. He had the gallantry of the Welsh, and then:

> I heard them sing,
> And loose the Celtic bird that has no wing,

No body, eye, nor feather,
Only song,
That indestructible, that golden thing.

His voice rang out, as praise, or as a heathen offering. He shared our home for some days. It could not have been simply on account of:

The little flower
That lights the palm into a nightmare land,
A bloody basin of the sterile moon,
That lights the face that sprouts the cigarette
Into a sudden passion of fierce colour.

There was no difference between us. Mervyn gave him a suit, and he went off one morning for a job, and never returned. He had said that if he didn't return he would end his life.

It is easy to be cynical.

★   ★   ★

Because of the fear of air-raids we gave up the flat in Maida Vale, and went to a cottage in Sussex in an ominously named hamlet called Warningcamp. The ancient Britons fearing a Roman invasion.

Our child was due within a few months. Mervyn received his call-up papers, and for us the war had really begun.

He had applied some time before for a job as a war artist, and had a testimonial from Augustus John, which he sent with his application to (could it be?) the War Office.

Dec. 28. 1939.

To whom it may concern.

I wish to recommend Mr. Mervyn Peake as a draughtsman of great distinction, who might be most suitably employed in war records.

AUGUSTUS JOHN.

Needless to say this made no impression on anyone at all, and he was sent to Dartford as a prospective gunner, non-commissioned.

*   *   *

The day that he left couldn't be imagined. We had never been parted, except for a few hours at a time, and during the time of the advent of our son, Sebastian. He was two weeks old when Mervyn had to leave.

Although it was winter, it was moderately mild. The hollowness that we felt at this first parting lingers still. It seemed impossible that strangers could so cruelly separate one. Until the last moment we would not believe it.

But the time for the train departure from Arundel came, and leaving Sebastian asleep in the cottage we walked together along the towpath, by the side of the river Arun, unbelieving, almost as though we had both been and were under sentence of death.

> Be proud, slow trees. Be glad you stones and birds,
> And you brown Arun river and all things
> That grow in silence through the hours of maytime—
> Be glad you are not fashioned in God's image.

Impossible to say goodbye, to contemplate a life apart. Mervyn made his way to an unknown world, and I, more luckily, back to the warmth of home.

When I returned to the cottage, under a tree in the front garden was a bicycle, with a note pinned to its handlebars.

A present which seemed the most extravagant I could ever receive. It had been put there whilst I was out by a neighbour, but was from Mervyn.

It was to be my only means of transport from the village to Arundel, with one and then two babies, for shopping. But I never thought of it as a bicycle. How could I have done so? I loved it, and for fifteen years at least in wartime and out it took me, my children, and my cat, with no effort along country lanes in England, and later in Sark.

To be separated after never having been separated is like losing a limb. The acute sense of loss. How can one know until one is deprived of what one has always taken for granted?

The dream had given way to reality. It was a soldier's world, no longer a world of words and paint. Words and paint were an interlude, and the excitement of our first child, first words, first steps, first tooth, could only be shared through the post.

> There is no other link—only the sliding
> Second we share: this desperate edge of now.

★ ★ ★

Mervyn wrote to say that I could come to see him in Dartford. I made arrangements to leave the baby, and arrived in Dartford at the arranged time. How strange that the compartment in which I had been sitting stopped exactly where a soldier was standing. A soldier who looked familiar, but unfamiliar. Deep-sunken eyes, a lean face, but where was the long black hair? It was explained to me: the sergeant-major had said, 'Get your 'air cut—you look like a bloody poet.' It would have had to happen whatever the sergeant-major had said. You have to do what you are told.

★ ★ ★

There was leave due, and we moved to another cottage in Warningcamp, where maybe the warning was a little less imperative. Not so close to the river, nearer a mysterious wood, with rides that no one used any longer, it always reminded us of Kipling's poem, 'A way through the woods', and in the autumn an abundance of blackberries for jam and bottling and picnics.

It was during this leave that *Titus Groan* gestated. Mervyn began to write it in publishers' dummy books. At this time it had not been conceived as a whole, it was a book that grew under duress. Mervyn had many of these beautiful publishers' dummies, which came to him mainly from Chatto and Windus, and Eyre and Spottiswoode. The very sight of them seemed to tender, generate and promulgate ideas as generously as a Roman Catholic in the face of a family planning clinic. After the leave, he took what he could in his kitbag, and left at home the first small book. Strange, how something as familiar to me now, familiar as one's first child, was not familiar, was something to be known, or learned, and part of one's life.

He was sent to the Isle of Sheppey to a gun-site. Gunner Peake 5917577. I feel sick when I think of the waste, but he was always without pride, without resentment. I think of the drawings he could have made, and the futile waste of talent, but perhaps he made more use of everything he saw and lived with than he would have done in any official capacity. How he survived the world of army discipline is incomprehensible. I think the answer is that he didn't survive it. Physically perhaps, but not mentally.

Letters of love arrived. The imminence of everything perhaps accentuated our love:

My Maeve, my artist-girl—companion of the years, the first of many a fire—my little honey-haired, golden-eyed sweetheart from whom I receive so much of my strength and all my love, take care of your sweet feminine self until I come back. I love you so much more than ever before. It is as though there were something richer and fuller in it, and something hotter so that when we quarrel, which all full blooded people do, it seems worse than ever, and when we love one another, it is more wonderful than ever.

After being on the bomb site on the Isle of Sheppey for some months, the Commanding Officer asked if any of the squad could drive. Mervyn happened to be the only man who could do so.

He was transferred not many days later to Blackpool. He was met at the station, almost as foreign royalty is greeted at Victoria Station, with red carpet and full panoply. He learned that he was to be the new driving instructor in a regiment of Sappers. Sapper Peake 5917577, driving instructor for heavy army vehicles.

His knowledge of an engine was rudimentary. He could make a car go, but more often than not it would stop without any instructions from him. It just stopped because it wanted to.

It seems that the Army is no more noted for its common sense than any other branch of human nature, but that is assuming the Army is human.

It must have been, for it took one hour precisely to judge that Sapper Peake had no intimate knowledge of the temperamental workings of heavy army lorries. He was demoted. His major task thereafter in Blackpool was to print elaborately beautiful cards which said 'Only officers may use this lavatory'.

I had a wire from him to say that he would be in Blackpool for some time, and that I could join him there when all the various practical dispositions of cottage and furnishings (such as they were) could be made.

A friend came with me to London with the baby, nappies and all the trappings of an unknown future home. I was put on a train for Blackpool, a compartment crammed with soldiers, and wives, or women, and sat in a corner with, even at the beginning of the journey, a very vociferous male child. I can remember the dress I was wearing. Bright red jersey, buttoned all down the front to make feeding easier, and I was sick with excitement.

It took fourteen hours to reach Blackpool. The train was blacked out and stopped over and over again, with no seeming reason, except once when the train was a target for a lone German raider. It stopped still with the dread that a gentle antelope might feel when mesmerized by a boa constrictor. In the ominous darkness, my son's screams seemed to beckon to that alien pilot, heard but unseen. It was almost impossible to believe that he could not be heard in all that quiet.

In the over-crowded compartment the soldiers were infinitely kind and took the wailing baby on their knees, sang to him in Cockney, or dialect: kind and witty and gentle.

The train at last arrived in Blackpool. It was *heaven*. Mervyn had waited hours. We went to his billet in Coronation Drive. It was a bleak arrival, around four in the morning, and it was not until the next day, after exhausted sleep, that I saw my future companions and the landladies of the billet.

We had a tiny room, and Mervyn spent most of his time pouring 'Nurse Harvey's Mixture' down our son's throat to silence what seemed to be a permanent siren-sound of screams.

We had meals ending with high tea about 5.30 in a dingy room that, on recollection, could almost have won a prize for being the drabbest one could conceive.

We spoke to a young R.A.F. man who was billeted there with his wife and child. He told us that he wrote poetry, and over the next four weeks we spent in Coronation Drive we

talked of everything that to him was a new world. Jack was his
name, and after we left he sent us the poems that he wrote. It
would be so easy, or it would have been so easy, to laugh at
them but I have them still. They fill me with a terrible sadness,
because he had the soul of a poet, without the knowledge. In
one letter he says:

> Please convey my deepest regards to Mervyn. I have much
> indeed to thank him for. Each day in its circle has spasm of
> reflection in my mind, that can always be kept apart from
> the commonplace happenings. This practice was first
> initiated by Mervyn, and I can interpret the ugly and the
> weirdest thoughts, making them adopt a deeper meaning
> than that which is seen only by the naked eye.

Jack was killed a year later over Germany.

*　　　*　　　*

Because of the very cramped quarters in Coronation Drive,
we applied for another billet. We were sent to one run by two
spinsters, and we had a bedroom and sitting-room, which
seemed almost immoral at that time.

Each morning I sat up in bed, polishing with Brasso the
regimental buttons, and Mervyn polished his boots until they
shone unnaturally. I wonder what his duties were during the
day? There could not have been all that number of officers
who were allowed to use those lavatories. There must surely
be a saturation point!

There must have been a war on somewhere, but it was early
days and it didn't seem to have found its feet.

In the evenings Mervyn wrote *Titus Groan*, and downstairs
one of the R.A.F. men played Glenn Miller. 'In the Mood',
'Moonlight Serenade', 'Pennsylvania 65,000'. It's a strange

association, but I still cannot read passages of his book without its awakening in me the sweet nostalgia of evenings which belonged to a nether world of waiting, a world that we all knew would end, and a world which hung suspended.

One day his Commanding Officer came to tea with us. He was not a Commanding Officer, but a man. Venerable in our company, unsure. He brought some of his poems and paintings, and he spoke of the loneliness and the deception of everything that he had felt was permanent, of how on his first leave he had returned to familiar places, familiar faces. After so short a time is one erased. People had forgotten his name and life had gone on. He simply felt alienated, and was glad to be back with his regiment. For a short space of time, for tea with us (and our 'little blossom', as the two spinster ladies in a thick Blackpudlian accent called our son) he was a human being with aspirations far removed from military splendour.

*   *   *

Although the war had not reached Blackpool, it seemed that a sapper who was no longer any use as a driving instructor to the Army was also no longer any use as a sign-writer for officers' lavatories.

The command came. Some remote authority thought it advisable that Sapper Peake should be transferred to the Lake District, where there were no facilities for wives.

Goodbye to Blackpool.

Near Warningcamp was a village on the Downs called Burpham, about three miles from Arundel. We found a thatched cottage at three shillings a week. No water inside, but a tap outside the back door. What a minute inconvenience!

I went to 94, Wepham, with Sebastian, and an imminent second arrival. Mervyn went to the Lake District. He was living in tents with a Negro regiment, and when he was free from discipline he walked and savoured the mystery of the district. It was, strangely enough, at this time that he was asked by Batsford to illustrate a book called *Witchcraft in England*. They sent reference books to him at the camp, and he illustrated the book, in the very vicinity where witchcraft still seemed to be particularly alive.

My sweetest, my most dear darling Maeve,

To-day you will be going into the Nursing Home. I have had no definite news whether I can come or not, but I will do my utmost. How wonderful it was to be able to talk to you last night, dear Maeve. As I told you I was talking from that family I told you about. They gave me high tea when I dropped in about 6 p.m., and I told them about you . . .

Maevie, I am in love. Deeply, un-endingly. For ever and ever.

Your Mervyn.

I cannot think how he found the materials with which to work, but he did, and produced a most marvellously vigorous set of drawings. The book was published within a year.

      ★   ★   ★

Apart from whatever he was doing on behalf of the war effort, illustrating *Witchcraft in England*, and writing poems, some of which were published in the *London Mercury*, the *Listener*, the *New English Weekly*, and the *Spectator*, his book was progressing as fast as a hunted stag. As each dummy book was completed he sent it back to me, and I kept all his manuscripts by my bed, together with a bagful of nappies in case of a sudden air-raid. Baby, books, nappies: the three most important things in life.

      ★   ★   ★

Where was the war? The countryside in Sussex was heavily beautiful. The downs, with their Piero della Francesca clumps of thorn bushes, were out of bounds. There was target practice, and fear of invasion made them especially venerable.

My second son, Fabian, was born in 1942 in 'The Peter Pan Nursing Home', and—is it possible?—a young nurse called Wendy looked after us.

Mervyn went to his sergeant and asked for compassionate leave, on the grounds of his wife having produced a baby, to be answered with 'What's so new about that?'

He forged a pass and came down for a brief visit.

It seemed when I returned to the cottage with Fabian, and Mervyn came home on leave, that there was a tenseness and a sense of withdrawal, that was shared and only partly shared. Perhaps the first time in our lives that we were not one. Was it the alien world that deprived one? It was certainly no loss of love. It grew and grew, but the world had intervened. A feeling of something amiss. To save the pain, he did not speak, but used the words that poetry alone can convey.

> O, this estrangement forms a distance vaster
> Than great seas and great lands
> Could lay between us, though in my hands
> Yours lie, that are less your hands than the plaster
> Casts of your hands. Your face, made in your likeness
> Floats like a ghost through its own clay from me,
> Even from you—O it has left us, we
> Are parted by a tract of thorn and water
> The bitter
> Knowledge of failure damns us where we stand
> Withdrawn, lonely, powerless, and
> Hand in hand.

*   *   *

Just after he returned to the Lake District, I had an official letter from the War Office saying that he had been sent to Southport with a nervous breakdown. It was six months before I saw him again, although we had desoltory phone calls and he wrote many letters, with drawings. One of the funniest was of him with his fellow sick-men queuing up for their meals, in long nightshirts, huge army boots, and cropped hair. They would then traipse back to their beds, remove the lumbering boots and sit up with their trays to eat—I wonder what?

His next-door neighbour in bed was a man who was also suffering from a breakdown. Being a spiritualist, he had been in the habit of receiving a visit from his mother (who had passed over) every evening at a certain time. On account of the Army time-table, she had never been able to find him, but in hospital they had been able to re-establish their old routine, and she came to see her son every evening at six o'clock promptly.

Because I know that Mervyn was unable to use his gifts as a war artist at this time I am flippant, and seek in the uselessness of Army life a joke. The only way to remain sane. Out of his breakdown he learned to make a bamboo recorder, and to play it. Unmilitary music, music like 'Plaisir d'amour', 'Jesu, joy of man's desiring', 'Parlez-moi d'amour'. A strange mixture of the serene and the sentimental. When he eventually came home on leave, his recorder was an essential part of him. I accompanied him on the piano, and once more nostalgia breaks through on hearing any of those songs.

*   *   *

After leave, following the breakdown and recuperation, his orders were to proceed to Salisbury Plain, for a course in 'theodolites'. I wonder whose strange twisted mind could think up so incongruous an idea. Certainly, although we had both heard of, and been to, Salisbury Plain neither of us knew the meaning of theodolite, and although Mervyn went to Salisbury on the course he never came any nearer to knowing.

At the end of the first lecture he asked to speak to the Commanding Officer.

He was allowed to speak, and explained that he felt he was out of his depth; that when, for instance, he saw a 6 or a 9, or an o, he always thought of them as female shapes, a 7 or a 1 as masculine, and he then asked permission to continue writing his book at the back of the room. He spoke a little of *Titus Groan*, and the Commanding Officer, who had been puffing at a pipe, removed it, cleaned out the bowl carefully with a pipe-cleaner, and then tapped it gently on his right hand. There was a positive sound of wood hitting wood. It *was* a sound of wood hitting wood, for his right hand was a wooden hand. He told Mervyn that until he could be transferred to another unit, more within his own world of thought, he might continue to write his book.

He *must* have been an enlightened man.

*　　*　　*

It was whilst on weekend leave from the theodolite nightmare that we decided to spend it in London. Mervyn had been lent a room in Frith Street. We found a kind friend to look after Sebastian in the country, and because I was feeding Fabian at the time we took him with us. His bed was like a beautifully made nest in the largest drawer of a chest of drawers, and we never even shut it by mistake.

We went on the first night in London to the Café Royal, where we knew an infinite number of people. It is a nostalgic memory, and even then we were always told by older people that it was not as it had been. Red plush couches and marble

The author, 1940

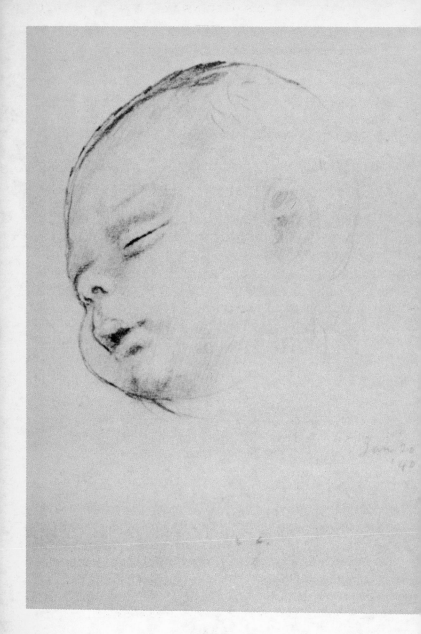

Sebastian, 1940

tables, and an evening spent if need be with just one cup of coffee. The elixir came from the lively minds of so many people now dead—John Davenport, Dylan Thomas, Roy Campbell. And on that particular night, Graham Greene. He asked Mervyn what he was doing, apart from being such a notable part of the war effort. Mervyn described, but not at length, the book he was writing, as yet untitled but possibly to be called *Titus Groan*.

We never thought again of that random conversation until a year or two later when Mervyn received a telegram from Graham Greene, asking him to submit the manuscript to Eyre and Spottiswoode of which he was then a director. It was finished and typed with great difficulty, as the writing became more obscure to read as the story proceeded.

Nevertheless, it was sent in typescript, and after some space of time was accepted in 1945. This is all rather after the time that I'm writing about, but it followed from our conversation with Graham Greene.

It was, or seemed, a miracle that a book written on compulsion, with no idea of publication, written as only, I think, true things are written, because it *had* to be, with no sense of future, past or present, that the message of interest came as a shock. A shock of complete amazement, that perhaps it would reach out, speak to people, make them laugh or cry, and in some cases hate, what had been written with an ebullience, a joy that the world of war in which we were living was trying hard to destroy.

The galley proofs which arrived were practically rewritten—ideas grew upon ideas on seeing in print what had been written in long-hand on those publishers' virgin dummy books. There was a tremendous sense of excitement, an almost impossible sense. We shared it. Those words, those characters written and brought alone to life, were to enter a world they knew not of, were frightened of, had no knowledge of. Like entering a party where one knew no one, and felt all around an animosity. Alien people, until you find that everyone else is frightened, then a sudden smile or joke invites you into their world.

*   *   *

Then the Army decided that Sapper Peake 5917577 was really no asset to them, and as he was on the edge of another breakdown he was invalided out, and sent home. He came back to Sussex, and after a week or so of rest he began his illustrations to *The Ancient Mariner*. Apart from making drawings of the children and myself everywhere, anywhere, writing poems, and doing illustrations for a magazine called *Lilliput*, we lived for a short space of time the life which had been interrupted in 1939.

Mervyn still had his room in Frith Street, and that is where the unique photographer, Bill Brandt, went to take some photos of him. It was a moderately sordid room in a moderately sordid house, and on the first photo the entire lights of the house fused. After a number of vicissitudes they were repaired, and one of the photographs appeared later in *Lilliput*.

Mervyn went to work at the Ministry of Information, and took a room in Store Street, close by. I've never been strong on facts or on dates, but I think it was through Graham Greene that he found himself in the Civil Service.

He had been commissioned to do two large paintings about this time. One was called 'The Glassblowers', which was shown at the National Gallery during the war. He went to Birmingham to do more drawings in the factory—the glassblowing was something to do with radar, and he made innumerable drawings. It was a theme full of fantasy and poetry, and the jacket of his book of poems called *The Glassblowers* was a reproduction of the final painting.

Another commission was done at an R.A.F. Bomber Station in Sussex. The scope for his imagination seemed less intense and he made a picture of The Squadron, small in a large space, which is now the Imperial War Museum. I think it interesting because it seems very untypical of him or his work.

He did drawings for propaganda leaflets, and was for the first time used in a small way as he should have been. I went to London from time to time with both the boys, although the air-raids were still a hazard. I have almost forgotten the fear in which one went to bed during those nights, and the wailing witchiness of sirens. How can one forget?

*   *   *

I remember standing in the garden in Sussex with both my sons, watching armadas of planes appearing from behind the Downs, disappearing towards the sea. A plethora of planes. Avenging angels. It was D-Day, only we didn't know it.

*   *   *

Past the rural flint wall of the cottage, with sunflowers straining over the flints, went columns of American soldiers, as curious as we were. Homesick men, who spoke and joked, and whistled at the two small boys astride the wall, playing with toy tanks. One soldier broke the line, and asked if he could visit me one evening. He came laden with chocolate and cigarettes, and spoke of home—the loneliness and fear of war, and nothing more. The *savour* of home.

*   *   *

This is not a chronicle of the war. It is trying to remember a lifetime ago. I am wishing to confine and savour a personal time amidst a public upheaval.

It was about now that the air-raids on London were

diminishing, and as our cottage, at 3s. a week, rates and all, was required by the Norfolk Estate, we decided to take a risk and return to London.

Mervyn had found a studio in Glebe Place, Chelsea, at a rent which seemed possible, for all the uncertainties of living, and we went to live there. A marvellous, spacious studio, with a few rooms as well for sleeping and living and cooking in.

We both painted. We had friends to coffee. It was cold, and one Christmas we were given a sack of coal. The ceiling was so high, and the studio was so large that there were always difficulties in keeping warm.

This was the time of the V.2s. Air-raids, as had been understood before, had changed their tune. Sitting huddled over the small fire with friends, talking of painting, listening to music, laughing or fooling, there would suddenly be a giant jerk, a reverberation, a jolt through coffee cups, then silence. Somewhere that crafty craft had landed, and ended someone else's laughter and tears.

The flying-bomb was also a part of our lives for a time—the sudden sickening stoppage of the engine, then the waiting for its arbitrary target. It wasn't bravery that kept one going, but the senseless faith that human nature has in human nature.

Mervyn wrote a long ballad called *The Rhyme of the Flying Bomb* a year or two later when everything could be seen a little more in perspective. It is very moving. A sailor in London during one of the flying-bomb attacks finds a baby, new-born but abandoned, and the ballad is his conversation and the baby's in the jagged burning city.

Just four verses out of a hundred or so:

> This isn't no place for the likes of you
> Nor it is for the likes of me
> We'd be better asleep in a hammock, we would
> On the wet of the mine-filled sea.

We'd be far better off where the soldiers are
Than naked in London town
Where a house can rock like a rocking-horse
And the bright bricks tumble down

All bare and cold in that gutter of gold
You had no cause to be,
No more than it's right for the likes of you
To be born in this century

But the sky is bright though its late at night
And the colours are gay as gay
And the glass that is lodged in my hip bone now
Is jabbing from far away.

*   *   *

It did end. It was coming to an end. Everything,
everywhere had that ominous feeling which portends something beyond our control. The fear which we had had for years
before the war had begun gave way, to an elation damaged
by the violence and the bestiality of which we had read but
scarcely believed possible.

The war in Europe was over. It was possible to go to bed at
nights without fear. There were still relatives and friends
abroad, who might still come to harm, but selfishly one could
not but feel a lightening of living.

On V.E. night some friends of ours, who had a young
baby, said that they would bring him round in a pram, and
stay with our sons, so that we could go up to the celebrations
in the West End.

A bonfire had already been lit in Glebe Place before we left
to meet some friends to go 'to town'.

I don't suppose one will ever feel again the madness of that
night, even though we knew there was still a war in the East,

and despite the knowledge that the end of a war is not really the end of war. It was not the time for introspection. Can I really believe that we danced the entire way up Piccadilly, linked with soldiers, sailors, airmen, tarts and the whole world? Singing 'Knees-up Mother Brown', laughing, crying, being kissed, kissing, until our voices were hoarse, our eyes closed with sleep and weeping, our feet swollen with dancing on the hard roads. Everybody loved everyone.

*   *   *

Such an occasion could inevitably only lead to an anti-climax. It came quicker for some than for others, but we were lucky in many ways.

Mervyn's brother, who had been a prisoner-of-war in Changi Gaol, Singapore, was alive and safe.

One day as I was bringing my sons back from a nursery school a taxi drew up outside our studio. A man got out of it with a kitbag. He seemed familiar, and he looked rather like Mervyn. It was his brother. I rushed up to him, and we wept. The taxi-driver would take no fare. Mervyn's brother met his nephews for the first time, and we went into the studio.

I had made some cakes for tea, and within a second they had all disappeared. He told us later that whilst in the prisoner-of-war camp he had dreamed not of esoteric meals but of bread and butter—always bread and butter—and these cakes were for the moment the nearest he could get to that. Because of his having been a prisoner we were supplied with extra rations for him, and in a modest way we were able to indulge him in all that he had missed over the last year.

It must have been traumatic to be carried from the harshness of Changi to the freedom of a studio in Chelsea. He stayed with us for several months whilst awaiting transport to

America, where his wife and family had been living during the whole time of his imprisonment.

*   *   *

The proofs of *Titus Groan* had been corrected, the book jacket had been designed, the blurb written, and we awaited the day of publication.

The very first review we saw was by a man called Edward Shanks. I don't remember for which paper he wrote, but it was a cold douche. Mervyn wanted to send a telegram 'Shanks a million', but we felt we had our pride. I can hear the people who level 'facetious' at his writing repeating it tenfold at this proposal. It *was* facetious, but also sad that the first review should have been starkly superior. He didn't send the telegram, and the majority of the reviews which followed were unexpectedly and fully in his favour. Since those days it has been called the literary sensation of 1945, but we still went on living, loving, working, fighting, in extreme ignorance of this fact. It certainly made very little practical difference to us. It was as difficult to pay the phone bill on being a literary sensation as before those august days.

Mervyn seemed able to swallow whole the good and the bad reviews. It's only now that I wonder if he really could, for it was cruel reviews many years later of a play in which he had placed too much hope that unhinged him in mind and spirit.

*   *   *

The war *was* over, but who could really pretend to themselves that life was or could ever again be the same? It is strange that Mervyn had to wait until it was all over to do the work which he had wished to do during it. He was sent with Tom Pocock, the journalist, to Germany to cover in drawings what Tom would cover in words. The nether land of horror.

Today we have been to the trial of Peter Bach. It was held in
a private house—a big one and about eight American
Colonels were the jury. I think it was carried out very fairly,
but the sentence was not read out. I made a lot of drawings
of the German witnesses as they came in and were
cross-questioned and of the German lawyer who defended
BACK—it is BACK not Bach as I originally thought. He (the
lawyer) was a huge, massive and portly man, and was I
think extremely good. Everything had to be translated into
English and German all the time, which made it very long.
He could not justify Back's action which he deplored, but he
tried to show the background which Back had had—how he
had been warped, and how being so self-conscious of his
being a cripple he had striven to excel himself as a party
man. None of this excuses him, but the lawyer quoted the
French phrase 'To know all is to forgive all'. Oh Maeve—it
was very tragic—its sadness is more upon me now than at
the time because the whole thing was informal in that big
room.

Tomorrow we go to Belsen.

He didn't write to me of Belsen, but I have seen drawings
and read poems.

They had no quiet and smoothed sheets of death to fold
  them, and no pillows whiter than the wings of Childhood's angels
There was no hush of love. No silence flowered about them,
  and no bland, enormous petals opened with stillness.
  Where was lavender or gentle light? Where were the
  coverlets of quiet? Or white hands to hold their bleeding
  claws that grabbed horribly for child or lover?
In twisting flames their twisting bodies blackened,
For History, that witless chronicler
Continued writing his long manuscript.

In *Titus Alone*, the tragic woman 'Black Rose' who has suffered so much, and died as her head touched a white pillow, after so many years, must surely be one of the lonely and forsaken ones whom he drew and wrote of from Belsen.

★   ★   ★

There were many letters at this time, full of a mixture of love, homesickness, hatred for the violence and havoc of war, and a yearning to be able to write and paint unaffected by outside events.

The river bank was alive with Castles—I've never seen so many—some of them perched precariously on precipitous crags or half hidden among the forests that topped the rocks. It was Grimm's Fairy Tales—a legendary thing. But in the river were tiers of boats and barges and steamers of all kinds and nearly all of them half or wholly under water, and along the road were all types of Germans pushing hand-carts or riding ox-drawn carts or pushing prams, each with the remains of their furniture. It seems to me that they are absolutely hostile.

A young heavily built German we passed gave us a look of the intensest malice, and clapped his hand to his hip as though to draw a symbolic revolver. The children put out their tongues to jeer and whistle. It is a new thing for me to see hatred so manifest. I also saw a boy whose face looked about sixteen, but whose hair was grey, who was hobbling down the steps of a town-hall with a crutch and only one leg.

War Correspondent,
C/o P.R.D.
Shaef

Most dearly beloved—oh my darling girl—

What a terrific lot has happened since I wrote to you from

Paris—yet I was in Paris this morning. I am now on the river near Wiesbaden, and tomorrow we are jeeping to Bonn.

After the impression I have received here of the way the Germans feel towards the Americans, and presumably towards the English too (we're in an American Zone at the moment) I don't feel too keen on introducing myself to one.

It is true that today a few peasants waved from the fields, and one or two oldish people bowed good morning and a few girls smiled hopefully, but in the main there is an intense feeling of hatred. Eyes are averted—or the stare is insolent. They are now doing what the Dutch, French and other subjugated races did when the Germans were in control. I have done today a drawing of a young Nazi—or Hitler Youth, wearing those strange short shorts—half way up the thighs and the sort of porter's cap they wear. It was the complete bully—rather impregnated with the spirit of Nazidom. The small children are openly cheeky or else when very young, cadging for rides on jeeps etc. Walking out this evening in this German town (Tom taking his revolver!!) was one of the strangest experiences I have ever had. Nearly every window had a head which stared at the opposite wall of the street as one came abreast. Sometimes looking quickly one would see a face staring at one from between the blinds, which would immediately shift its gaze on its being met. We are right on the river which is very wide but not particularly attractive near here. One or two people canoeing and a lot of boats and fishing nets on the shore. Also a line of our invasion barges which were used for crossing the Rhine. But the main part of the town—a very big town—is like Mannheim (to which we flew this morning). Sights which it would be impossible to believe were one not to see them. They are no more. They are relics. Terrible as the bombing of London was, it is absolutely nothing—nothing compared with this unutterable desolation. Imagine Chelsea in fragments with not one single house with any more than a few weird shaped walls where it once stood, and you will get an idea in miniature of what Mannheim and Wiesbaden are like—yet these are the only two that we have seen, save for the broken streets of every small town we passed through on our jeep ride here today. The Ruhr to which we are going tomorrow is reputed to be the worst—but how could it be worse than what I've seen today.

There were many letters, but the main content was always the tragedy of the human condition—'I must never let anything get cold'.

You know I will do all that is in me to do what was in our minds when we decided, through your insight, that it was for me to make records of what humanity suffered through war. I will not forget the reasons which prompted me to try and go to where people suffer. I will miss you desperately, but I will be proud to do something which we both believe in. . . .

During this time, apart from the horrors that he was seeing, and the nightmare, there was another side to life. In Hamburg he met the Old Vic Company who were touring and playing to the troops. Laurence Olivier was playing Richard III, and Mervyn did several drawings of him as the hunchback king, of Sybil Thorndike, and of a host of other actors and actresses lending truth to 'All the world's a stage'.

In Paris, where he went with Tom Pocock after Germany, they went to night clubs where people were emerging from the chrysalis of war. Negro drummers, angels and gargoyles. Part of a Paris known before, but changed as everything had. As he had. A shadow, a man with a shadow.

★　　　★　　　★

He was away a month, and during that month the sights and sounds of Germany must have damaged him more than he ever said, except in his poems and his writing in *Titus Alone* many years later, and his drawings. Perhaps there was the seed of all this in his work—he had 'grotesque' used about most aspects of it from the time he started—but there is also tenderness and humour, which the myriads of drawings of children express, and the lyrical poems contain.

* * *

It was around this time that Mervyn met John Brophy. He came to the studio, and overwhelmed us by buying one very large oil, and several drawings, and leaving a cheque that seemed over-life-size. He was a most genial man, always kind and with humour. He became a very good friend, and remained so until he died.

There was a shelf out of reach in our studio where coins were thrown, of any denomination, at the end of the day. It needed a great deal of athletic prowess to recover them at the end of the month, but each time it was like opening our Christmas stockings. We didn't know what we would find, but it is surprising how quickly pennies and half pennies, and their more wealthy relatives, sixpences and shillings, even florins and half-crowns, become a small fortune when left on the shelf. Covered in dust they become a revelation.

The Peter Jones of 'negative' repute decided to become patron of the arts. They opened a gallery, through the dress materials and the haberdashery departments. We were both asked to exhibit self-portraits. This was one of the first exhibitions to be held there, and a strange happening arose out of Mervyn's self-portrait.

The exhibition was at a time of year when it was excruciatingly cold, both inside and without, and there were layers of multi-coloured snow outside the studio. The front door was directly on to the road.

It might be apposite to describe the painting. Mervyn had a face that belonged to another age. Cadaverous, romantic (women thought it beautiful), haggard and wild. He had painted himself with a paint-brush through his teeth, as a pirate might hold a cutlass, or a gypsy dancer a rose. It was a painting of bravura.

*   *   *

The exhibition opened, and a few people went to look at the pictures, but in the main the public were people matching cotton to the materials they had chosen, and marching intrepidly towards the large window to see if they had correctly chosen their pinks, or yellows, or greens. A slight glance to left and right gave on to a world that had no meaning to them, and they walked with upright steps back to the security of the world they knew.

But somewhere amongst the people who saw this painting was someone to whom it was an insult against aesthetics and beauty.

The evening of the private view (it was not private, but perhaps a view) was icy cold, but we went to bed around midnight, warming each other as well as possible. Presumably we went to sleep, but around 2 a.m. we both awoke with a sharp instinct of fear. Our bed was on the same level as the front door—it was not a bedroom but an alcove. There was a sound, a rattle at the letter-box, and muffled steps running, in the snow. They could only have been muffled because of the silence of snow. At the moment that the letter-box rattled there was a piercing scream from a room at the diametric end of the studio, where Sebastian was sleeping. Who was to do what? I ran to my son, and Mervyn to the front door.

I found a small boy, frozen with terror, pointing to a window where the curtains were pulled tightly across, so that there was no possibility of seeing out of them, or into them, screaming of an old woman who had been peering through the glass. There was nothing, and no possibility of anything. I tried to calm the little creature, but waited with trepidation to hear what Mervyn had found at the door. To begin with, a wire had been stretched across the door, which would have cut a thoughtless throat, but he had withdrawn in time, and on the doorstep was a loaf of bread made into a face—currants (predictably) for eyes, and through where should have been the mouth a paint-brush.

I was trembling—the whole thing seemed unclean and devious. We called the police, and in our large, cold studio explained to them the sinister sound of padded footsteps, the wire, dirty collars full of congealed bacon-rind pushed through the letter-box, our son's insistence on an old woman. In cold blood the most strange details take on a prosaic quality, and after the policemen left it seemed quite obvious that nothing out of the normal had happened at all.

It was cold though, and before we could return to bed we had to calm down the boy who had seen the old woman through heavy curtains.

*   *   *

It was a few days later that the police again came to see us.

The widow of an R.A. who had seen Mervyn's self-portrait, had hated it so vitriolically that she could only think of doing harm to someone who, in her eyes, had desecrated *art* and her husband. The strangest thing in the story was that our son had described this old woman at the back of the house through drawn curtains when she was busily thrusting bacon-rind through the letter-box at the front.

*   *   *

People of all kinds came in and went out of our lives at this time. One weekend, whilst I was away, Dylan Thomas arrived at the studio, far from well. Mervyn put him to bed, the same bed that had witnessed the old woman's fury from the inside-out. The doctor came, and administered whatever there was to be administered—it almost seems like the blind leading the blind, but whatever remedies were suggested must have had some effect, for he recovered and left. Mervyn had done some drawings of him in bed, two of which were reproduced in *Encounter*. They were never returned to us, as they had been lost in the office, although, according to a letter from Stephen Spender, Mervyn hadn't asked for them back until a year or two after their publication. They did make an *ex gratia* payment of £25 for the drawings.

Not long after the blind leading the blind, a note was pushed through the door.

Mervyn, dear Maeve,

   Will you please lend me coat and trousers for a day. Any coat and trousers so long as they aren't my own. I am supposed to speak on a public platform tomorrow, Sunday, just after lunch. May I call early morning—

Love, Dylan

On the other side, with a scribbled drawing:

I must, unfortunately, call for coat and trousers—doesn't matter that M is taller than D before 11. Say 10.30.

M was quite a bit taller than D, and a fair bit slimmer, and D had the look of a tortoise coming out of its shell in M's coat and trousers. Where the public platform was and what he spoke about are both conjectural.

       *   *   *

It was still impossible to believe that the days and the nights were silent from bombs. It is hardly credible that for six years going to bed was a query whether we would be there to get up. And because of the easing of life, life itself became more wondrous.

'To live at all, is miracle enough.'

It seemed so, that each day was a leprechaun—humorous and fanciful, adventurous and mystical.

It was a time for us, if only we had known it, when the world was bubbling. It was a time when Mervyn, particularly, met new and not new people. Important people! Our world was our cocoon, but I had no wish to meet anyone—turpentine and canvas, words and a pencil, paper and paint—my love.

Around this time I had an exhibition at the Redfern Gallery. Looking back, I wonder how I dared exhibit any of the pictures. It wasn't arrogance or confidence, but a kind of blindness.

Mervyn too had an exhibition at a gallery called the Adams Gallery, but he had a habit of painting over his canvases so that any which were not sold were completely metamorphosized, and the shapes beneath became the shapes to dominate the new painting. Strange, that above all things that he did he wished to be a painter, and I think it was perhaps the medium in which he was least sure.

We came to know Maurice Collis then, and he remained to me over the long years of Mervyn's illness someone to whom I could turn, and whose humour and wit sustained darkness and despair. But the days when we first knew him were happier and we met with him a new world of people. A little later Mervyn illustrated his book called *Quest for Sita*, which was a beautifully produced edition on hand-made paper. Rare for those days when wartime economy was still extant.

Fabian, our son, was known by a little girl at the nursery

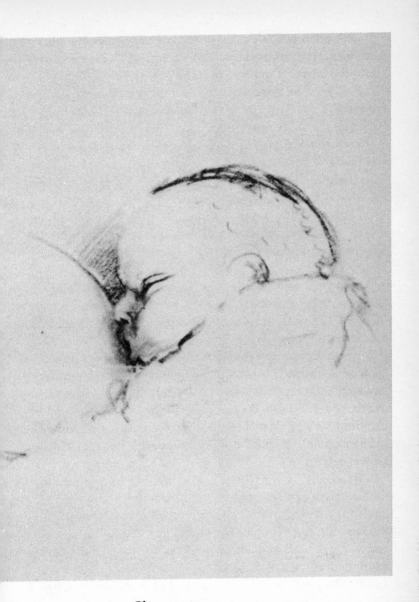

Clare, 1949

Blue-eyed thugs, 1943

school as the 'pinky-orange boy'; he had an angelic face which belied great mischievousness. One day when I was fetching him from school I watched him putting his arms gently round the little girl whose mother was standing close to me, and we were both sentimentally touched by such sibling sweetness, until a moment later it was shattered by a shrill scream. A large slice of tender cheek had been bitten into by the pinky-orange boy. Relations were never the same again.

Our two sons, who were later described by Louis MacNeice as 'blue-eyed thugs', lived wild lives with us in our studio. Mervyn would draw them at any moment, playing and fighting. We took them to the zoo, to tea-parties, where Fabian would lie anti-socially in the corner and speak to no one. They met Prince Lowenstein, son-in-law of Victor Gollancz, in Kings Road, and have never got over the shock of his head that sported no crown. Mervyn took them for walks along the river, and at low tide they took off their shoes and socks and paddled in the muddy slime, to return home smelling of all the unmentionable things that a river exudes.

★   ★   ★

Titus seemed to be selling; and one day Matthew Smith came to our studio to look at paintings. He was, in my memory, a very gentle man, and it seemed difficult to equate his personality with the rich and powerful pictures that he made. Mervyn gave him a copy of *Titus Groan*, and later on received a letter from him.

Dear Mervyn Peake,
    I felt it indeed a privilege to have a copy of your book. I
· am deep in it and entranced. I consider it a masterpiece. It
    must live.
    That wonderful foot that you manage to keep on the

ground! Thank you for a Gargantuan Feast and at the same
time an escape. So bless you and thank you.

> Yours,
> Matthew Smith.

Not to have illustrated it is alone a stroke of genius!

*   *   *

Although we had this big studio, a place for working in, we
longed to go away.

Mervyn had been given a retainer by Eyre and Spottiswoode to illustrate a certain number of books a year, and he
had many other ideas swimming and floating in his
ever-active, lively brain.

He went over to Sark to look for a house for us. He had
always felt a great love for this small island, since 1933, when
he had spent one or two years there, as a very young man, after
finishing at the Academy Schools, and where he had exhibited
in a most unlikely gallery.

*   *   *

Eric Drake had taught Mervyn English at Eltham College,
in Kent, and I think was a very positive influence in his life as
an artist, poet, and novelist; he decided to build a gallery in
Sark, and to start a colony of artists. It was a revolutionary
idea, for such a small island, $3\frac{1}{2}$ miles by $1\frac{1}{2}$ miles. The gallery
itself was something unforeseen in so remote a place. 'The
Directors do not subscribe to any set theory or school of
thought . . . they are looking for work that has a constructive
and integrating significance in modern life.'

Reviews galore appeared in the Channel Islands papers, and
one perhaps foreshadowed the future in the *Guernsey Press*.
'An outstanding exhibitor is Mervyn Peake who won the

Hacker Porticut Prize at the Royal Academy Schools in 1931, and has exhibited at the Royal Academy, the Redfern Gallery, and the London Group. His chalk and charcoal studies of venerable Sarkese are masterly. . . .'

'The standard throughout was on a particularly high level, and in some cases the work was stamped with something approaching genius. This was particularly so in the case of Mervyn Peake, a young man still on the sunny side of twenty-two whose versatility and imagination place him in a class of his own. . . . Mr Drake is very proud of the fact that it was whilst teaching this boy literature that he discovered his ability to draw, and encouraged him.'

Mervyn spent a few years in Sark in a small tin shack with a pet cormorant, painting, writing and living, and taking midnight swims in the beautiful lonely bays, and was then offered a job teaching at the Westminster School of Art by the principal of the school, on the strength of his drawings. He decided to take it, and to leave the island, despite all that he loved—and but for that we would never have met.

*   *   *

Sark, after the turmoil of the war, seemed to be a sanctuary, although it had itself been occupied by the Germans, and many people had been deported. Towards the end of the war there was a great deal of hunger among Germans and Sarkese alike.

He came back, full of houses that he had seen, one in particular, too large, comparatively ugly, but with immense space—a daffodil field, a bamboo hedge, pampas grass, no light, no electricity, no water, except by pumping, but alive, alive, with rooms for possibilities, and a whole island to explore.

We went together, after arranging for the boys to be looked

after, to see Le Châlet. It seemed a most inappropriate name. A large ungainly house, not endemic to the island, built by an elderly widow from England, used to better days and a staff of servants.

We saw it as an ugly house, prepared for anything, prepared above all to be lived in and worked in, loved and hated. Houses, like people, have their own peculiarities, and we both loved the peculiarities of this one. I've always thought of it as a spinster house, ready and willing to be invaded.

Mr Hirzel Baker from Guernsey was the landlord. The terms were £80 per annum for a ninety-nine-year lease. I think we were all completely unbusiness-like. We were getting what at the time was a white elephant, and he was getting rid of it. I don't *think* there was anything so ungentlemanly as a lease, only I can't remember. It was mutually agreed that at a certain date we would take possession of this ageing spinster, then after a few days staying and talking, walking, swimming, dreaming in Sark, we returned to London to dispose of our commitments, and to start thinking of living in an island where life was lived at a tempo unmolested by cleverness.

A small diversion: whilst Mervyn was away in Sark for the first time, someone living nearby tried to convert me to Christian Science.

During this short period when I was alone I happened, over a very trivial matter of opening a glass jar of boot polish, to get the glass into my thumb, and a jagged, bloody mess of skin hung suspended from my thumb. I had my small sons with me, terrified at the horrible sight, so I hurried round to our Christian Scientist friend, and asked him to look after them whilst I went to the doctor. His reply was, 'If that has happened, you must be guilty of a great sin. I'm sorry, I cannot help you.'

I rushed round to the doctor with my hand aloft, bleeding decoratively down my arm, like a Tachist painting, and on the

way, met a white—I don't mean non-colonial, but colour-
less—friend who seemed not to notice the gall, and would
have kept me in conversation for many minutes, if my *sang-*
(*chaud? froid!*) had not forsaken me. I rushed posthaste to the
doctor's and had six stitches put in the thumb, with two poor
little white-faced boys even more pallid. It was at this moment
that I decided not to embrace Christian Science.

★ ★ ★

We were about to move into a house with at least twelve
rooms from a studio that was comparatively under-
nourished. What should or could we do? Nothing, just decide
to go.

Our belongings were put into a pantechnicon. A railway
van that would go oversea to Guernsey. Our cat, an essential,
was to come with us.

★ ★ ★

I don't forget. I never will. All that was beyond what we
were doing. A man with a family who is also a man with
enormous creative impetus, works in a different way from a
bank-clerk, a financial tycoon, or a film-star. Maybe he
doesn't, but Mervyn did.

It's a beautiful sight, arriving in the early morning, by ship,
at Guernsey. The islands are mysterious, slowly coming to
life—seal-like shapes, in a mist, and the fog-horns and
sea-gulls add to the hallucinatory aura. It's a pity to land so
prosaically, and to make one's way up the 'Pollet' for breakfast
before taking the boat over to Sark. One should always be
defended against reality.

★ ★ ★

Our cat had survived the journey with the first of her nine lives. We took a small boat with an outboard motor to Sark. I can always remember the excitement of trailing hands in the water, it was a calm day, and the shape of Sark slowly materializing, magically, no reality anywhere. Beautiful silence, except for the engine, the lapping of the sea against the boat, and the intermittent excited cries of children enjoying something quite new. They had seen a school of porpoises, gracefully submerging and reappearing, they had seen cormorants and puffins, and they saw looming ahead of them a shape that was to become for ever a part of their lives.

We landed, and were greeted by many of the Sarkese, who had known Mervyn for years, since his days as a painter, exhibiting pictures, unworried by family ties.

There were no cars, only horse-drawn carriages for everything. We were drawn up to our house by Charlie Penée, who later drew Princess Elizabeth up the steep harbour hill, and had a royal coat of arms painted on his carriage. I don't think such an honour ensued from us!

*   *   *

Our furniture was to arrive the next day, so we arrived at a house devoid of everything except space.

There was no light, no beds, no food.

We were given candles, and bread and butter. We slept on the floor.

It was a strange first night. Although it was a young house, it had an old feeling. As darkness fell and the wind rose, in the flickering candlelight the ghost of Mrs Judkins (who had built it) did not walk, but whispered as we all slept on the floor of a big bedroom from which the coast of France could be seen. Her whispers subsided as the dawn rose, and we were all only too happy to arise from the hard floor.

Our furniture, pathetically minuscule as it was, should begin to arrive around eight in the morning. It all came, by horse-drawn carriage up the harbour hill and into our drive, a beautiful sweep of bamboo, and up to the front door. Paintings, paintings, paintings. Singly they arrived in Victorian carriages. A little later, we heard that there had been a large-scale exhibition of them on the quay in St Peter Port, Guernsey, before they were put into the motor-boats for Sark. Oh, how I wish we could live those days again.

At the end of the day we could hardly say our house was furnished. We had one couch, two beds, a few chairs, books and books, two large easels and a host of drawings and paintings and work-to-be.

The excitement of two small boys let loose on an island with no cars was limpidly pure. To run wildly and exhaustingly nowhere in particular.

A strange, sharp little woman came to see us, and to say that she would do housework for us, as she had for Mrs Judkins. 'Gracie' from Derby (she pronounced it D*u*rby), with a wit, humour, and maliciousness all her own. It was she who told us of all the sales in the island, after the occupation. We bought a kitchen table, with which I could never part, for ten shillings, beds for £1, carpets for I can't remember how much, and suddenly our house was furnished. Beautiful oil-lamps and heaters and a bookcase with supports made from tea chests. It was a home, and work could begin again.

*　　　*　　　*

Sebastian was old enough to go to the school in Sark, just next to the prison, which features in a book called *Mr Pye* which Mervyn wrote after we left the island. Both the children made friends with the Sarkese boys, and I can think of no more exciting childhood than that which they had. We had a donkey, called Judy, aged thirty, and it was Gracie who told us of a little carriage to be auctioned, with bridles and accoutrements, that we bought for a pound or two, and to which Judy was harnessed with no great willingness on her part. She knew how to open the kitchen window, and nuzzle the lid off the bread-bin, which stood on the sill, and go off with whatever bread she could find. A few years later our sons used to harness her, and take visitors to the island on journeys round it for a few shillings a time.

*   *   *

People used to say, 'What can you do all day? *what* do you do? what *can* you do? there's nothing to do.'

There was a world to do.

*   *   *

Mervyn woke, and either went downstairs if it wasn't too cold, or to his room to write. *Gormenghast* was progressing. Books were being illustrated. We were both painting. Or if it was cold, he wrote in bed until about twelve noon. We all had breakfast in bed together, then Sebastian would run down the hill to school and Fabian would sit and draw for hours.

Mervyn never sat alone in a study to write or draw. He hated to be cut off from the life going on in the house, and in his manuscripts of *Titus Groan* there are drawings of the children or of myself caught suddenly in an act of living. He often sat in an armchair with a drawing board across its arms, and no more props than those which came from his superabundant imagination. Some days he wrote more easily than others, but as the story unfolded he read it to me.

It is very strange that although to many people he is mostly known as a draughtsman and illustrator, I cannot now read his poems or his books without their evoking in me a more intense sadness than his drawings. I hear him in every line and every thought, in every humorous and extravagant fancy. The tenderness that was germane to him and the quality of clowning.

★   ★   ★

Every day was new. From our bedroom, on mornings when there was no sea mist, we looked out on to the coast of France. The trees, apart from those in the Dixcart Valley, a sheltered valley in the centre of the island, were warped by the wind into strange, grotesque and sometimes ghostly shapes. I loved to paint them, against the sea, and their loneliness. Mervyn wrote a poem because of them:

> With people, so with trees: when there are groups
> Of either, men or trees, some will remain
> Aloof while others cluster where one stoops
> To breathe some dusky secret. Some complain
>
> And some gesticulate and some are blind;
> Some toss their heads above green towns; some freeze
> For lack of love in copses of mankind;
> Some laugh; some mourn; with people, so with trees.

★   ★   ★

At times the gales surrounding the island became so insistent that one longed for silence, the uncanny silence which sea-mist carries, but the eerie sound of fog-horns was a poor substitute for it.

There were moments when I particularly felt an intense claustrophobia, knowing that in whichever direction one went there was the sea, and one was trapped.

These feelings did not last very long, although there were

times when no boats could come from Guernsey with provisions or mail for a week or two at a time.

The days, weeks and years we spent in Sark were perhaps the most memorable of our life together. Our sons had their friends who were born and bred on the island. Our garden was large and wild, with a field of daffodils in the spring that could have inspired Wordsworth, and the freedom from fear of car accidents allowed the children to run like leverets where they wished.

Apart from a few months in the winter we used to go for picnics down to one of the many bays—with lonely stretches of beach, mysterious caves, rocks to climb, in some of the bays amethyst and topaz to be searched for, but never found.

We walked everywhere, although I still had my bicycle and used it quite often for all the paraphernalia of picnics. Our cat, called Chloe, often walked with us to the top of the bays, and would wait for our return.

Once a week there was a film in the hall. Very old films, George Formby, Will Hay, and once, Deanna Durbin with whom Sebastian fell in love.

The cheapest seats in the front row were benches, backless and hard, but the group of small boys in the front row were agog with excitement, and practically always asleep by the end of the film. They had to make their way home across a cemetery, not really knowing a great deal of what they had seen in the film, but thrilled to be out so late; and frightened by the grave-stones they ran as fast as their tiredness could carry them.

* * *

Judy, the donkey, often made her way into our sitting-room, and would stand for hours in front of the bookcase. A most intellectual donkey, who spoke little, and never disgraced herself. Sometimes, visitors who had come over from one of the other islands for the day, would drop in to see us, and found her a somewhat unusual hostess, one who contributed by her presence alone to the niceties of hospitality.

This was a time of great creative energy and inspiration in living. *Gormenghast* was growing and each day I longed to know how the people in it were progressing, sadly, tragically, humorously, over-life-size friends.

Although the book was the major concern to be finished, apart from a fairly modest advance, which must surely have been spent before being received, money had to be found to enable us to stay in Sark. Mervyn went over to London from time to time to keep in touch with the fount of finance.

He did a series of advertisements for the Brewers Society, which must have helped financially, but it didn't last long, as so many things extraneous to the drawings were always queried. I remember one drawing of a young couple sitting outside a country pub which was returned as unsuitable. The tree under which they were sitting with their tankards was apparently too close to the inn, and would thus have undermined the foundations. The tree must be placed further away. The uprooting of the tree was, perhaps, easier in a drawing than in nature, but it decided Mervyn to uproot himself from the Brewers Society and to look elsewhere for means of support.

He was illustrating *Treasure Island* for Eyre and Spottis-woode, and some of the caves in Sark were inspiration for Jim Hawkins on his lone adventure. Sebastian or Fabian would be asked in the middle of some wild game of Indians with their friends to pose in a tree as Jim, or with me as Blind Pew, covered in an ancient coat and transformed into the sinister man of Stevenson's book. They posed moderately willingly so long as their game was not interrupted too cruelly and they could return to the wonders of the Sioux before the tribe had been completely wiped out.

On one of his visits to London, Mervyn had become fascinated by toxophily, and he returned with very beautiful equipment for us all, bought from Lillywhites. It was a new word for me, and unpronounceable for the boys, but getting to know more about it added yet another dimension to a life already over-flowing.

Bows and arrows, a target, quivers, shields for the fingers, it was a magical idea. We set the target up in the garden, at the bottom of the daffodil field, and it was certainly more through luck than skill that the arrows didn't fly over the hedge and into an innocent horse or man or woman or child. I had very little talent for toxophily, although it is such a graceful achievement if done well. Our Red Indians were infinitely more adaptable, it being a major part of their lives, and Mervyn had the surety of eye that his draughtsmanship had instilled in him to hit the bull's-eye.

*   *   *

Grimm's Fairy Tales, also for Eyre and Spottiswoode, was being illustrated, and once again we were all called in to pose—Rumplestiltskin, a witch, a sprite, a queen, a princess, in a rage, laughing, holding a scythe, whatever was necessary to transform and fuse imagination and reality.

Whilst Mervyn did his illustrations, in the evenings, after the boys were in bed, and he sat ensconced behind his drawing board, trapped by it and the fine mapping pens and Indian ink which he used, I read to him: *Bleak House*, several other Dickens', *Candide*, *The Loved One*, a catholic selection.

The days were too short for all that we wanted to do. The two boys both went to school, and returned for lunch. Every lunchtime Mervyn did a drawing for each of them in a special book. Pirates or cars, boats or tigers, in coloured inks or water colour or pencil or pen, and off they would rush back to school with the intensity of excitement that only children feel. Even then, they both had to have extra lessons in mathematics—a subject which always eluded them, as it always had their parents. A complete blank, that world of numbers. Eight is a woman. Seven is a man.

*   *   *

In front of the house there was quite a wide gravel drive, and in front of that a lawn which called for decoration. Horticulture seemed to have got into our blood. One day Mervyn phoned a nursery in Guernsey and asked them to send a palm tree over to us in Sark. They were not surprised by such an order, but needed specifications. What kind of palm tree? A momentary hesitation, then a silence, then, we would ring back. We rushed to the *Encyclopaedia Britannica*, and searched for palm trees. I no longer have an encyclopaedia, so I cannot remember what exotic species it belonged to. It was shipped over from Guernsey, and arrived, a huge spiky, furry trunk, with all its hands folded over each other inside thick sacking. A deep hole had to be dug in which to house it. It spent its first night on the lawn, and was the next day heaved into its new home, where it seemed to sway unsteadily, as land-sick as a tree can be, until it finds its roots.

It was a sanctuary during the years we spent in Sark for our cat and our sons who climbed it as easily as monkeys, to survey the land and sea-scapes surrounding us. After we left the island, and the house was sold, it was one of the first things to be removed. Poor palm tree.

The other grandiose scheme we had for garden improvements was to make a pergola, but no ordinary pergola. Telegraph poles were being lopped down in the island, and Mervyn thought that they would make a pergola of wondrous proportions. We bought twelve poles. It took about six men to struggle with them into our garden, and to drop them like giant matchsticks at the side of a hedge, where they lay discarded and uncared for, with no more thought of being a pergola than a pergola has of being a telegraph pole. They stayed silently there until we left a few years later.

*   *   *

Louis MacNeice, whom Mervyn knew in London, asked if he and his wife and children could come over to stay with us, and they all came with their Italian maid one stormy day. He only stayed about three days, as he had a telegram from the B.B.C., recalling him for a programme that he was working on.

*   *   *

These were little asides of life. Not highly successful, but enough to know that gardening was not our *métier*. The over-life-size pergola, burgeoning with honeysuckle, climbing roses and wistaria never materialized.

We went to dances at the hall, which were primitive and generous. We left Gracie from Durby to sit in, and she smoked non-stop. She herself did the can-can whenever she felt like it, with enormous Northern vitality, high-kicking, red bloomers ahoy, and she cleaned our house with the rapidity of a lynx, and the cleanliness of a cat, garrulous and comical.

She went to all the sales, of which there were many in the island at this time. She bought a small carriage with its accoutrements for our use with the donkey, a beautiful Victorian case for drawings, which she gave to Mervyn, oil-lamps of ornate design, and a life-size lay-figure which, apart from being a period-piece, has served as a surrealistic prop in the home, a silent figure reading the paper, with gloves on its hands and a mute personality of its own.

Just now, during 1949, our third child was on the way, and when Gracie was told she left—she couldn't bear babies. We asked our sons to guess what surprise there was for them. One guess was a pig, one a bicycle, another a parrot or a monkey, all of which we would like to have had, or a dog. It never entered their minds that such a thing as a baby could possibly be of interest to them, and the reception of the news was greeted with very little enthusiasm.

Materializing almost from the sea-mist came Armand, who had heard we wanted someone to help us in the house. His real name was Ahmed Ben Ali, a Moroccan who had come to Sark to work on the building of a new harbour, and he wanted to stay in the island. He was a kind and infinitely gentle man, and we decided mutually that we all liked each other, so he would come to do garden and housework for us.

*   *   *

The months went by. *Gormenghast* progressed. I painted every afternoon, mostly the wild trees and boys surrounding us.

We exchanged a drawing of Mervyn's for six Khaki Campbells. The vicar wanted the drawing very much, and suggested a system of barter for it. We had never had ducks before, and had felt no blank space in our lives because of the absence of them. I imagined this particular species in kilts, and waking up in the morning to the sound of bagpipes, but they proved to be khaki-coloured ducks with very little talent for anything except laying eggs in out-of-the-way places. None of us really liked duck-eggs, even when we could find them. By elimination, we gradually found the things for which we were not suited, and keeping ducks was another. Nevertheless, we had no inferiority complex on this account.

Sometimes Mervyn, the children and I all played follow-my-leader round an intricate box hedge in the front of the house on an array of bicycles and tricycles, trying not to fall as we rounded the corners.

It was not far from *Titus*, this world where the mist hid one from another, and the wind howled as violently as the scarecrow dogs in the outer dwellings of Gormenghast, and the fog-horns wailed as one could imagine 'The Thing' in her melancholy. It grew, and progressed as much a part of each day as eating, sleeping, and making love. The children, and the advent of our third child, were interwoven in everything which Mervyn did. His manuscripts are filled with drawings of us all, in the moments when words ceased to flow and the pen or pencil took over, a child with a bow and arrow, screaming, laughing, or myself sleeping. Illustrating, writing, walking, climbing up trees and down to remote bays, watching schools of dolphins, hearing the screech of sea-gulls, puffin landing, all of this world entered everything upon which Mervyn embarked, and my own painting could not but be touched by the wildness, the beauty which surrounded us.

* * *

There was no hospital on Sark. A good doctor, but no midwife. I wanted to stay at home to have the baby, so we arranged for a nurse to come from England. She arrived, and must have been horrified at the absence of amenities. Most of her clients had been titled ladies, and indeed her only subject of conversation was the royal family, about which we had only rudimentary knowledge.

Mervyn had to go down first during her stay every morning to inspect the sitting-room. Quite often there were the desiccated remains of a rabbit or a bird or a rat brought in by our cat during the night, and left as a matter of pride in the middle of the floor, but when you have been used to stately

Boy on a donkey, 1948

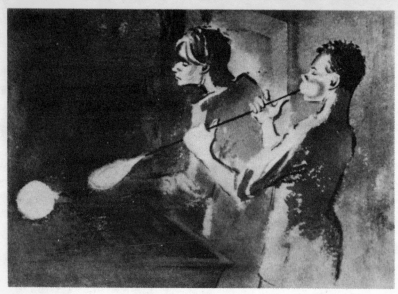

Sketch for the Glassblowers, 1944
Sketch in Yugoslavia, 1953

homes you must protest at this anti-social lack of behaviour.

On account of some miscalculation, the baby arrived two and a half weeks late, so that we began to grow quite acquainted with the ramifications of the royal family.

During the days of waiting, in order to try to hasten the advent, I went for long walks with the nurse, and because she happened to have rather larger proportions than even I had, I pulled her over stiles and hedges, and we went for drives in one of the Victorian carriages over the uneven roads, with Fabian sitting up in front by the driver. Often he would turn round, particularly after a very bumpy patch, and ask if the baby had come yet.

It almost seemed as though everything was a mistake, and there was no baby due, but one night there were the unmistakable signs. Mervyn woke the nurse, and was told to put a blanket to warm on the Aga cooker, and heat some water. I thought of all the Western films in which these mysterious preparations were made. Soon there was a gentle smell of scorching, and the blanket carried until its end a circular patch imprinted on it by the hot-plate.

Mervyn took his book and a pen, and went to another room where he said he would write. I went to my painting room, and started painting a still-life, which under the circumstances doesn't seem quite appropriate. I walked round the house from room to room, hardly believing that within a few hours there would be a new life in it. All the platitudes one knows crowded through one's mind, of birth and living and death.

The nurse kept asking if I was having a good pain, and as time progressed the answer was more often in the affirmative. I dropped in to see Mervyn more than once, and found him in a deep sleep, pencil in his hand, his manuscript dropped on the floor.

At eight in the morning, a girl arrived and Mervyn was awakened to be told that he had a daughter. I can still hear

Armand shouting to the vicar's wife, whose house was at the end of our garden, '*C'est une fille. C'est une fille.*'

★   ★   ★

Things were pseudo-hygienic. Face-masks were an essential. I saw Mervyn soon after the birth when he came to see his daughter. He said that she looked like Winston Churchill, which nearly reduced the nurse to apoplexy.

In the afternoon, the door was pushed open and he came in, maskless, with a painting, still wet, that he had done to celebrate the birth. I hardly caught sight of it before he was pushed out of the room in a most irate fashion and told not to return without a face-mask, and certainly not with such a germ-laden anachronism as a huge canvas of three kindly monsters sitting at a table. In the eyes of the nurse there seemed to be little relation between the baby and the picture.

At nights, my cat used to creep stealthily into the room and sleep on the bed, until early morning when Mervyn removed her.

★   ★   ★

I had written to the parish priest in Guernsey a month or two before the time due, to say that I would like my child to be baptized at home, as it would be difficult to go to St Peter-Port with a new-born baby. There was some delay in receiving a reply, and when it came it was to say that a special dispensation had been granted, as normally it is only royalty who are baptized in their own homes.

A day was arranged for a priest to come, and Mervyn went down to the harbour to meet him. It was a day of gales, and perhaps that priest is nearer heaven for having wrenched one unbaptized child from limbo, at the cost of his own nausea and

sea-sickness, than he might have been at the more normal
baptismal font. He was ushered into our living-room, where
the donkey awaited him. He seemed to have very little taste
for whatever was offered in the way of nourishment. The
main object was to make a Christian of the small pagan
upstairs as quickly as possible. The ceremony was held in the
bedroom, and Fabian, who had seen his sister Clare for the
first time, was transfixed by the unreality of the object. He
could only find it in him to laugh, and to compare it with the
Khaki Campbell ducklings, which he infinitely preferred.

*   *   *

Unless one has a positive means of income, it is difficult to
live on an island, away from the people who can make it
possible for an artist to survive.

Dawning gradually was the knowledge that the life we were
leading would have to change. There was not enough money
coming in, and yet looking back we lived with no
extravagance. The extravagance was the life we were living.

*   *   *

We made up our minds that we would have to leave, but
before doing so we went over to stay in a farmhouse in
Guernsey, where Sebastian was now at school. We wanted to
show him his sister also. His reaction was slightly different
from his brother's. Apart from the daily routine of lessons, he
and his friends spent all their free time exploring the dug-outs
left by the German occupation, finding bayonets, helmets,
German hieroglyphics, and then, as is the way of boys,
fighting pitched battles with their dangerous trophies.

How can a new baby compete with such wonders?

*   *   *

In the autumn of 1949 it was time to go. Our wild garden with the bamboo hedge, the scene of so much living, our house, with so very few conveniences, but full of work and loving. We left it, our lease unexpired, returned to the landlord for the next ninety-five years.

We had to go back to London, where there was work to be found, for painters and a writer. We found a flat on the Embankment overlooking the river, and began to try not to miss the expanse of freedom that we had known on Sark. There was water, and there were trees, and nearby the Royal Hospital Gardens in which to stretch one's limbs.

Our sons were still at school in Guernsey, so that we had just the baby and the cat.

Mervyn began teaching life-drawing at the Central School of Art in Holborn, which gave us some basic money, and then he began to work on many other ideas. A collected book of poems was due to be published, called *The Glassblowers*. It covered many of the poems during the war, and afterwards. As mentioned earlier, the long poem from which the book took its title was written during and after the visit to Birmingham to the glassblowing factory, which seemed to have given him great inspiration. He described the glassblowers themselves as having the skill and self-discipline of ballet-dancers, and yet at the same time because of the distortions that their faces were subject to they had the dedicated look of trombonists or trumpet players. Mervyn seemed to see many things in terms of ballet—one of the least likely perhaps was cricket. Before taking me to the Oval once to see a Gentlemen *v*. Players match, he described to me the ritual of the game, the archaic terminology, the movements of a dance, a poetic and incomprehensible language to a novice. It seemed to me that nothing happened all afternoon, except a repetitious act of throwing a ball, and someone at the other end managing to hit it or miss it, and at intervals an interchanging of men in white to other places on a green field.

Rugby, too, he saw as a ballet of violence. Perhaps ballet is really only a game of cricket, with different skills.

*   *   *

At this time we met many actors—Esmond Knight, who had been partially blinded in the war, and his wife Nora Swinburne, Cyril Cusack, with his Irish wit, and Anthony Quayle. A liveliness descended.

By 1950 Mervyn had begun to think in terms of a play. His over-abundant mind was excited by the idea of the theatre and the vivacity of the actors whom we met stimulated his ideas. All the same, it was not until a year later that he began to write a play, which had a desperate bearing on our lives.

It was as though the years in Sark were needed for refuelling, and now once again we were in a hectic world, meeting people, and being able to know of the latest films, books, paintings, plays. An island is full of natural violence, which does not prepare one for the violence of people.

*   *   *

We happened to be living above the flat of a middle-aged couple with a girl around the age of our second son. The mother took some violent dislike to me, and would wait at her open door until I came down, then slam the door shut with the dreadful omnipotence of the righteous as I passed her. That is the kind of thing which can turn one into some kind of neurotic, but we simply decided to move. Later, the poor daughter was murdered, and the murderer, a middle-aged man, was tried and found guilty.

Glancing through the *Sunday Times*, we saw advertised a house with studio in Kent, and we decided to look at it. I had been left some money by my mother, and it seemed that life in a flat in London with three children was not an ideal existence for them.

We went to see 'The Grange' in Smarden, Kent. It was a Queen Anne house with an orchard and a cottage where studios could be made, with long hot-houses and vegetable patches. It was not an artist's house. It was a house for a gentleman with visible means of support. Why did we take it, I wonder? Looking back, it is impossible to know, except that the slamming doors had begun to make too great an impact on our lives.

*   *   *

Neither of us had the slightest idea of leases, of the vicissitudes of borrowing money. We were warned against it, but we did it, and an incongruous cavalcade of paintings and people, children and cats, arrived to take up residence in this very beautiful house.

Mrs Bull, a lady who had worked for us in Chelsea, came with us, to help us settle in. She developed a boil, and Mervyn a carbuncle. It took a little time to attend to each, but somehow furniture is moved, paintings and books take their righteous places, and one becomes a member, even for a short time, of a community to which one does not belong. The boys went to the village school and learned a great deal about birds' eggs, although their mathematics still gave cause for great alarm.

We had far too much property. An orchard that would only disintegrate unless properly attended to. We let it, and sheep and pigs grazed in it, but we had the freedom of it, and at the right time of year were able to pluck for our modest demands plums, or apples or pears or mushrooms, if one was able to distinguish them from toadstools. None of us died.

We had picnics in the orchard, and were awakened by green-woodpeckers outside our bedroom window. *Gormenghast* was published, and on 4 April 1951 a letter came, which was perhaps the most beautiful that could arrive.

I remember standing in the hall, whilst Mervyn read it to me, as I wept. Why do tears always spring up so readily? It was from the Royal Society of Literature.

> I have the honour to inform you that my Council wish to award you a prize in respect of your novel 'Gormenghast' and your book of poems 'The Glassblowers'.

£100 was to be ours, free of income tax; his wonderful world had been entered into, and lo and behold I still weep. We were both as thrilled as one was at school on receiving an award for good behaviour or French.

*　　　*　　　*

A friend of ours, an artist, whom we had not seen for several years, had discovered our address, and arrived one day with an English wife married in Italy. The last time we had seen him he was desperate at Churchill's parliamentary defeat after the war. He was now a communist, and also, after the year of being in Italy, had no home and no work, only a burning desire to paint. We suggested that they should come to stay in the cottage, where I had a big painting room, but it was self-contained, and could house a man and woman and several score of paintings. We stayed a year in our completely anachronistic house, and they stayed a year in the cottage.

It was they who suggested they would look after our children, whilst we went to Paris on the proceeds of the £100 award.

We went, and stayed in a hotel in Montparnasse where it

was said that Oscar Wilde died. It had no particular significance, as it had been recommended to us by someone who had never heard of Oscar Wilde, but who knew that it was moderate in price.

How sad life is. I was bitten by fleas on our first night, and awoke looking like a balloon. Mervyn went out to get some dark glasses, but even they couldn't hide the unsightliness, and such is the vanity that besets one that I wouldn't leave the room until the ointments had done their work, and I had attained a certain resemblance to *moi-même*. After this it seemed that we should flee (?!) from Paris. Small childish humour has always appealed.

We went to a place called Montigny-sur-Loing which was, as its chief claim to fame, the habitat of a film-star called Michele Morgan. Staying in a modest pension, we walked and slept and drank red wine, enough to enable us to join Alcoholics Anonymous. The only memorable thing at Montigny was a walk at midnight along the deserted lanes of the village, *alongside* and, thank God, *inside* a wire fence, accompanied by the insatiable panting of alsatians who longed to break loose from the fencing, but man had been too cunning and they were confined, only able to violate us at second-fence.

On our way home we stayed again in Paris, and saw a few of the things which had been our purpose in the first place: Le Jeu des Paumes, and the Louvre.

*   *   *

We returned home. I, personally, am not one to be transplanted too often—Mervyn less so—but the banners and flags, the laughter and tears, of our welcome was enough to eschew any further absence.

Because the train journeys were infrequent to London, and

it was essential for Mervyn to get there in time to teach, we decided to buy a car. It was a momentous decision. Mervyn had a licence to drive, and I had just enough money to buy something on four wheels. Even in 1951 it was difficult, and we had to know someone who knew someone. We eventually found someone who knew someone, and a car was to arrive, at a certain time on a certain date. Our sons had been told. To them, the mystery of the advent of a car was a hundredfold more thrilling than the advent of a prospective brother or sister. I think we all expected a winged chariot, a miracle, a humming-bird, but what we actually saw was a black beetle, a thing of shreds and patches, a Wolseley, down at heel, and having lived its life to the full. It was tired, worn out as an old nag. It had little left to give, and to the two with dreams of speed it could offer nothing but crutches. We never ended a journey we had begun in it.

★ ★ ★

Such is the life of a man alive with an intensity of living. A year before, a book called *The Drawings of Mervyn Peake* had been published, to which he wrote a Foreword that included the following:

This is the problem of the artist—to discover his language. It is a lifelong search, for when the idiom is found it has then to be developed and sharpened. But worse than no style is a mannerism—a formula for producing effects, the first of suicide.

 If I am asked whether all this is not just a little 'intense'—in other words, if it is suggested that it doesn't really matter, I say that it matters fundamentally. For one may as well be asked, Does life matter?—Does man matter? If man matters, then the highest flights of his mind and his imagination matter. His vision matters, his sense of wonder, his vitality matters. It gives the lie to the nihilists and those who cry 'WOE' in the streets. For art is the voice of man, naked, militant, and unashamed.

*   *   *

I was painting a great deal, during the afternoon mainly, when Clare was asleep, tethered in the orchard to a sheep, and before the return from school of the blue-eyed thugs. It was just now that Mervyn began to write his play, as yet untitled. He became obsessed with the theatre. Esmond Knight came to stay with us, and it was read to him as it progressed. Being an actor of long standing, *and* a friend of long standing, he gave his opinions with forthrightness and courage.

The playwright who wrote *Strange Orchestra* and *The Old Ladies*, Rodney Ackland, also came for a weekend, but his first night was marred by the presence of a bat in his bedroom.

The drama society of Smarden put on a one-act play of Mervyn's, and it was then the nearest we had come to hearing words made in silence publicly pronounced. Of all mediums it seems to be the nearest to a public examination of conscience.

Being a parochial affair, there was no fear of being hurt. It was elucidating, thrilling, and the sight of the two boys sitting in front, yet again on hard benches, swelling with pride at their father's prowess, was almost more rewarding than the play itself.

*   *   *

There were oast-houses attached to the farms surrounding us, in which cider was made. A cider to knock one out. We had an American acquaintance who wanted to come to see us for the day. Mervyn met her at the station in our miracle car.

With old-world courtesy he saw her into her seat, and as he shut the door all the windows slid softly open. A three-mile journey was ahead, and unless one had foreknowledge one would expect to make it without 'let or hindrance'. A gentle wind stirred, enough to lift the sunshine roof and see it float unhindered over the fields and faraway. Perhaps our trans-atlantic friend should have been ready for anything, but on being offered a glass of cider, and yet another, she tossed it down uncaringly, with the indifference of one used to pink gins and martinis, and before long she was safely tucked up in bed where she stayed a day or two, the purpose of her visit never really materializing. A book to be illustrated, we believed.

*   *   *

Flippancy is the only weapon I have against tragedy. It couldn't be foreseen, but it was on its way. Tiny manifesta-tions, not yet identifiable, but there was still time for joy.

Mr Pye, a story based on Sark, was begun now. It was written truly, but also in the hope that it might make some much needed money. How could we know that it would be remaindered? The hope and the enthusiasm were there, the pleasure and the difficulties of its growing, like children, the impossibilities of seeing which way it would go. Seeing ahead wouldn't have mattered in any case. The important thing was to make something, and to hope.

From Smarden, on 4 April 1951, we went up to the Royal Society of Literature for Mervyn to receive his award. Although I have already written of the fruits of this, I have not mentioned the ceremony. There was a lecture, and a speech by R. A. Butler about the book, and afterwards we were introduced to him, and Mervyn was made a Fellow of the Society.

To have public confirmation of something which one already knows is perhaps vain, but none the less a happy experience.

*　　　　*　　　　*

Everything seemed to be a mixture of so many things. Trying to make enough money to live on, but at the same time painting pictures which might never sell, writing poems for which, even if accepted, the remuneration would not be over £2, and the book, *Mr Pye*, progressing. Mowing the lawns that surrounded the house which we should not really be living in, too big and too expensive it was. Going to watch 'The Golden Arrow' flashing by at a certain time each day was a major event. Talking about painting to the artist who was living in our cottage, drinking cider in neighbouring farms, seeing the hops flower, the miracle of the orchards, a variety of birds to watch, and hear the woodpecker like an alarm clock outside our bedroom window punctually every morning tapping away at the bark, bats and a white owl flying at night, with all the mystery that whiteness endows on the earth, on beasts, on all that it inhabits.

One night Mervyn stayed up late, and around three in the morning he woke me to say that he had started the play which had been in his mind for some time. He had the title for it, *The Wit to Woo*, and had written for about four hours. He was tremendously excited, and read to me what he had written, and also outlined the theme and the story. There *was* a certain amount at this time to keep one's mind active.

*　　　　*　　　　*

There was a general election, also, to make life less exciting. It happened that the artist's wife (in the cottage) was pregnant and imminently so, on the day of the election. In the early hours of the morning after polling day, we were awakened by the gentle sound of small stones hitting our window, and a voice calling out what seemed to be 'Labour's in—Labour's in'. As none of us was heavily interested in the result, it seemed a little unnecessary to wake us up in the middle of the night to give this information. From a drugged sleep Mervyn managed to get to the window, and to open it in a kind of trance. The solitary figure was standing on the lawn, in the moonlight. The election, it slowly dawned on us, was not his major concern, but his wife who was *in* labour, and he had come to ask if he could borrow our car to drive to London, to the hospital where all arrangements had been made. The necessary keys were found, and thrown out or handed over, and a little later in a mist of sleep we heard the uncertain sound of our car, idiosyncratic and unreliable, on the road, puffing past our house.

The next morning, the woman who came to do our cleaning arrived, with red eyes, which became redder and more swollen as the results of the election became manifest. The midnight prognostication had not been correct. In fact, nothing of that evening had been correct. The car returned, with no baby. Everything had been a false alarm.

★   ★   ★

A man we knew was organizing an exhibition of children's book illustrations for spastic children, and Mervyn was asked to contribute. He sent several drawings, amongst them one for *The Hunting of the Snark*. The exhibition was to be opened by the Queen, and she was also asked if she would accept one of Mervyn's drawings.

The place where the exhibition was held was unbelievably incongruous, in the basement of Gorringes in Buckingham

Palace Road, through the garden furniture department and the hardware. Not having seen or been close to any member of the royal family before, it was a matter of curiosity. The main thing I remember was the officiousness and bumbledom of the tail-coated members of the staff and entourage, herding the viewers into sheep pens, probably from the gardening department. Mervyn was given a little more respect as he was to be presented to the Queen, but his attire was perhaps not in the highest echelon of sartorial excellence, and therefore the respect was perhaps a shade less obsequious than to those of more perfect appearance.

It may be that I was prejudiced, but it seemed to me that in this dour world of handshaking and petty exchanges, as the Queen went down the line of bowing and handshaking, her eyes lit slightly as they came upon Mervyn. I know mine would have, but then I wasn't the Queen.

*   *   *

It slowly dawned that buying a house which one couldn't afford was not the way to make money. Apart from the fact that the bank had begun to query everything to do with us, we knew that once more it was time to go. Money is something we simply did not understand.

The house was put up for sale. Anyway, it hadn't belonged to us. It had been there for years before we went there, and it will be there for years to come, so little impact does one make on the history of a house.

In the meantime we continued to do all the things that we were doing anyway. Mervyn was finishing *Mr Pye*, and writing his play, at full speed ahead, painting, mowing lawns, teaching. (Oh Jesus, take me away.)

We went to Ashford, the nearest market town, to shop, and pulling up near a bus stop we saw a policeman watching us. I think to say with the eyes of a hawk would be a compliment to the policeman but, watching us sharply, and the moment that we had come to a stop, parked the car, and gone to wherever we wanted to go, up he came to Mervyn, shoulder tapping, and asking to see his insurance, and his this and his that. We had nothing. We thought you bought a car, and that was that. I know better now. Beautiful insurance, it was.

The policeman had never heard of people who had never heard of insurance, and road tax and licences. We were told to go to the nearest police-station, and our story was so ludicrous that we were let off whatever it was that we should have been guilty of, on condition that we armed ourselves with all civilized impedimenta such as little round discs on the front of the car to prove that we were worthy, and bits of paper for insurance to prove that we were even worthier.

We used to drive to the woods in Smarden, where there lived a tramp entirely dressed in newspaper. The woods were his home. In them he lived, slept, ate, and did everything else that is necessary for a human being to do. The smell from his black cauldron was delectable. We never spoke to him. His privacy had something sacrosanct in it. To have invaded it would have been crude to a degree. He had a natural courtesy, and dignity, and said good-evening with all the gentleness that one thinks nuns should be gifted with.

*   *   *

It was a beautiful part of the world in which to live, but too beautiful when our foolishness became manifest. All the wise people had been right. Not only could we not begin to pay anyone back for the house, we couldn't even pay the interest, which was something only just beginning to be understood by me. I think Mervyn had no idea, and never would have, what interest meant. It was just to be interested. . . .

So the house was put up for sale. Naturally there was some kind of financial crisis in the country, and although we sold it after a time it was at a loss of far more than we could have envisaged, but that follows the pattern.

We put most of our furniture into store, the same familiar but well-lived-in possessions that had survived so many moves. We went with our paintings and some books, our cat and our children, to a studio we had had for many years in Chelsea. A studio which had been found guilty in the First World War, but which had stayed its course until well after the second one. There are not so generous gifts to painters now. It was a studio such as no longer exists, except for people of very large incomes. Somehow or other we all managed to live in it, when the two boys were on holiday from school in Guernsey. We had a kind of little tent within the studio for our daughter, so that in the evenings when she had gone to bed and our friends came to see us she would not be disturbed. It was rather exciting to have a miniature room within a room.

In some ways it was one of the happiest times, apart from Sark. Our only possessions were those which were an integral part of us, books, paints, canvases, chalks, turpentine, and a few necessities, such as a bed and a chair or two, and enough plates and so on to make it possible to eat.

Mr Pye had been accepted and was about to be published, and the writing of the play was taking a great deal of time. Mervyn was placing too much hope in it. Above all things he wanted to prove to himself that he could make money. He wanted to give us all exotic and strange presents. He wanted to *feel* a success. Why did he feel that in a medium less known to him than his own pencils and brushes and pens he could achieve this? I suppose because the fruits of success are more possible in the theatre, if they are a success, than the sale of a painting, a book of poems, or his own books, which had achieved *succès d'estime*, but financially less than any manual

German Boy, 1945

A young Welsh coal-miner, 1938

work could earn. Why did he? Oh why? I've always hated the theatre since those days, the even worse cruelty that can be inflicted by critics on a man who works in silence, and displays himself in public, than the disinterest that a painter receives from the public. What is made in silence, out of passion and craftsmanship, should not be displayed until long after the passion has died away.

★   ★   ★

Although the lack of possessions was a kind of release, with children growing and needing to stretch their limbs, it was obvious that the five of us couldn't live for ever in a studio meant for one artist or two, in one huge room with a black monster of a stove, pipes of gargantuan proportions, ugly stove and beautiful warmth, and painting and drawing in progress around. It isn't the life for boys, although our daughter was now going to the same nursery school as the two blue-eyed thugs or pinky-orange boys had gone to a decade before.

Mervyn's father had died a year ago, leaving us a big Victorian Gothic house in Wallington, Surrey. In its way it was monstrously ugly, but as is the way with monstrously ugly things or people it was endearing, as is a mongol child to its parents, as all physical defects become endearing when one ceases to notice them and loves the bearer. And that is neither facile nor easy to say.

★   ★   ★

We went to look at this house, to see if it were possible to become a part of it. Personally, I loved the house, and hated where it was. It was spacious. It had at least twelve or thirteen rooms, with strange mysterious attics where the water tanks had lives of their own. A large garden, a garden where twenty-five years ago Mervyn had played tennis. Tennis parties on the lawn, almost a world of Bertie Wooster, where his parents had lived on their return from China, where his father had built a practice, and a home, far from the world and the aspirations that he had known and groped for. How far removed was this world from the Boxer Rebellion and the medical difficulties of Tientsin!

And yet again, how far removed was this world before the war from the world after the war. To most people this house would have been a castle; and yet, to Mervyn's parents, who were of very moderate means, it was a normal place in which to live and work.

It really was not a matter of a decision for us. It was a matter of when to go, and how to go. No one we knew in Chelsea could believe we were in our right minds if we could banish ourselves to the suburbs. Sark has an elegance about it. Wallington has not. One can be eccentric, but only in a certain kind of way.

*   *   *

Arrangements for schooling were made, and one dreadful day all our even more dreadful possessions made their appearance in this strange Gothic pile (and this was long after *Titus Groan* and *Gormenghast* had been so castigated).

The misgivings of possessions are manifold, especially when they have no intrinsic beauty. The thing is perhaps to have less and less, and only the things one wants.

In the seven years that we spent in this Outer Siberia, I can think of only two people to whom we talked. I spoke to hundreds of people, I fetched my daughter and took her to school each day—my sons were at another school—but the aridity was frightening. There was a nothingness, more than the claustrophobia of being surrounded by sea.

We had children's parties for Clare, and one mother on fetching her daughter looked at the paintings and drawings everywhere, and said, 'Oh yes, I dabble too.'

★   ★   ★

The Wit to Woo was finished, and as Mervyn had met Laurence Olivier and knew him slightly he was the first person to whom he thought of sending it for an opinion. His letter in return was not encouraging:

> . . . original and extremely good as is most of the writing I rather fear that the 'Crazy' (horrid word but I can think of no other) theme, is a highly dangerous one, and the audience is apt to get rather irritated by it. I remember we had them stamping out in a rage many times in 'Skin'—a play which was masterly both in its construction and in its writing and packed tight as a drum within its own fold—play convention.
>
> Also the rhythm in your writing together with the sort of verbal and onomatopaeic (spelling?) joking is trickily reminiscent of Fry and I do fear the sensation of its being derivative from both this author and Wilde and falling rather short of matching the content of either.
>
> Forgive me please if this letter steps over the bounds in the way of frankness, but I admire you so much indeed that I cannot but be entirely honest with you.

This was the beginning, only we didn't know it. Or should I say this was the end, only we didn't know it. I think it's almost appalling that human nature does go on hoping, and believing against all odds that everything is for the best in the best of all possible worlds.

I read *Candide* to Mervyn as he was illustrating *Alice in*

Wonderland. A peculiar juxtaposition of fantasy, originality and Gallic coldness and logic.

In the midst of living, working, eating, loving, fighting, a tiny little manifestation of shaking hands began in Mervyn. We treated it as a joke—too much drinking, only he was a moderate drinker, too much work, and that he certainly did to wonderful excess. He began in a small way to tire more easily than usual, to sleep whenever possible, to shake a little.

A wonderful friend of ours, who had known Mervyn since the days when he taught at the Westminster School of Art, saw him in this condition and gave us money to go to Spain for a holiday. The fares, the hotels, and enough to leave for the children whilst we were away if satisfactory arrangements could be made for them.

We thought he was over-tired, strained, we still had a noble overdraft from our foray into Kent, the effort of living, and the effort of working, trying to, oh God knows what.

The world seemed to be a series of cold douches. It did seem to be a time to go away. Spain had always been somewhere that we had both wished to see. Goya was the man and the artist that Mervyn most admired, Velasquez, El Greco, other miracle workers, apart from the world of flamenco, and horribly, perhaps, bullfighting, poverty and wealth.

*   *   *

We did make arrangements for the children, and of course our cats. They were dispersed, happily and adequately, and we left strange suburbia-land for Madrid. For a short space of time our finances, although in our hands, had been put away by another's. There were people since the onset of Mervyn's disease, who used generosity and imagination, and this was the first, and most unforgettable, occasion.

Dry, red, and arid, we landed in a country of small, dark

men. Not the romantic place of singing and carefree laughter. At least, that is how we saw it. In many ways bleak and lacking the fantasy of London. But then, why expect to find what one has left behind?

We had been given introductions by friends, one particularly to Walter Starkie, who lived in Madrid, and was a Hispanophile. Naturally, before all else we wished to go to the Prado, to see, it almost seems in the flesh, the paintings, etchings, cartoons of Goya, the magnificence of Velasquez. El Greco, the myopic original, whose paintings made Mervyn write a sonnet to and for him:

> They spire terrific bodies into heaven
> Tall saints enswathen in a frozen flare
> Of twisting draperies that coil through air
> Of dye incredible, in rapture thriven
> And heads set steeply skyward, brittle-carven
> Again the coiling clouds in regions rare;
> Their beauty, ice-like, shrills—and everywhere
> A metal music sounds, cold spirit shriven.
> So drives the acid nail of coloured pain
> Into our venerable wood, earth-rooted,
> And sends the red sap racing through the trees
> Where slugged it lay, now spun with visions looted
> From whirring skies and cold Gethsemanes
> Of bitter light, and all the wounds of Spain.

The Prado was closed to the public for the time that we were in Madrid, being redecorated, and we thought that fate had made this decree at that particular moment out of some dreadful spleen, and we would not see Goya.

We had been asked to Walter Starkie's apartment to meet him and his wife, and were made encouragingly welcome, given a great deal of highly knowledgeable information, and above all an introduction to the curator of the Prado. We arrived with our letter and spent nearly a day there, alone except for an elderly attendant who escorted us, and who clearly loved his canvas protégées. I think his intense devotion to them and his knowledge was one of the most touching things we encountered in Spain. Love always does touch one, watching it in others, whatever or whoever is the recipient.

Despite the wonders the world has to offer, to me the greatest wonder is two people loving each other in their own world. Nevertheless, this isn't the way to see Spain. One has heard of the proud people, the poor, the rich, the beggars, the gypsies, flamenco, caves, bullfighting, Holy Week in Seville, but how can one expect to encompass all within three weeks? Even in one's own country, how does one ever come to terms with the dreadful anachronisms that sway one backwards and forwards?

I cannot write a travelogue of Spain on three weeks' knowledge. I can say we were horrified by the poverty we saw outside Madrid, thrilled by the grandeur and the surrealism of Escorial, frightened and excited by the bull-ring, curious at the extent of the richness of the sea-foods, the octopus, the over-life-size prawns, tired of veal, exhilarated by the genius of castanets and heel tapping so fast that it almost becomes motionless.

We met Lady Lindsay Hogg, who had been an actress called Frances Doble. A beautiful Englishwoman, with a fanatic love of Spain. Mervyn did quite a few drawings of her, which he gave to her. She took us to parts of Madrid which we would never have otherwise seen, and one evening we were asked to meet her and a group of eccentric Americans at the Ritz. Certainly we would never have found our way there—not even to the Ritz in London. We all had dinner at an exclusive restaurant, with very Spanish dishes, and afterwards went on to a small private bull-ring just outside Madrid. A matador called Miguel Osta arrived with his entourage, one member of which brought his guitar. The patron of the inn, which belonged to the bull-ring, a huge man with an enormous paunch, sat on a wooden chair, singing flamenco almost as though one could see his heart, so passionate was the song, or the series of songs that he sang, with tears flowing down his cheeks.

After the singing, the matador staged a bullfight with the wicker bull's head that adorns so many walls in Spain. With immense grace he dedicated the bull to me, and went through the gestures and movements of this barbaric and courageous play. He had with him the ears and the tail of a bull that he had killed that afternoon. How does one ever reach decisions about one's feelings over bullfights? I wish I knew what I felt about everything, but gradually one realizes that one has no definite feelings about anything. I've always hated violence above everything, but watching a bullfight one is lured by its very beauty which encompasses violence to man and beast. But the argument against it is of course that it is man-made, although man also stands a strong chance of physical damage.

After the evening in this obscure and beautiful white-washed bull-ring we were taken home, or rather back to our hotel, in the bullfighter's enormous black car, with all his equipment piled high on the roof. It seemed to me that he had almost transformed himself into the bull, and we charged at the traffic on two wheels, until the moment of truth, when we came to a stop outside our destination, around three in the morning, when one claps for the concierge to unlock the door. I found clapping one's hands for service very feudal.

We were asked to tea by some grandees to whom we had been introduced. I think it was tea as a compliment to us, but it was at eight o'clock at night, and we were admitted to the silent and opulent house by a flunkey wearing white gloves. The courtesy and the formality was from another world, and the aloofness of our host and hostess did not warm us. There was a magnificent collection of Spanish paintings, and of French impressionists. Wealth has the power to awe one, especially when accompanied, and I think it nearly always is, by a withdrawal from the prosaic things of life.

We were led to the dining-room, where an English tea had been prepared. We sat formally and silent, waited on by immaculate white-gloved servants. When the mistress wanted something, or saw that we had need of marmalade or bread, she clapped her hands autocratically, and our needs were attended to like the flick of a serpent's tongue.

We went to Toledo, and saw El Greco's house, his easel, and the skies around which were his paintings. Avila filled Mervyn with horror, at least the convent where St Theresa had lived and prayed away from the world, and where one of her fingers was on display, with a magnificent ring upon it. It seemed a gruesome relic, but then there is in Spain much emphasis on the blood and the suffering of Christ.

*   *   *

We returned to England with various trophies for our children. A veil and roses, and a dainty small lace bag for our daughter's first communion, knives from Toledo for the boys, and a batch of drawings that Mervyn had made. Subjects ranging over many aspects of Spanish life, the ubiquitous priest, the blind lottery sellers, the young army recruits in their far-too-long greatcoats, particularly as they seemed always very short men, donkeys, which are endemic to Spain, and columns of Falangist boys. One or two of these drawings were reproduced in *Encounter*.

*   *   *

Spain had revivified us, and the strange tremors that Mervyn had been heir to were less. Our hope was renewed. Life began again. Teaching at the Central School of Art, becoming more and more immersed in his play, the conflicting reactions to it from people who could influence its coming to life in the theatre.

It had been revised and rewritten, as is the way with people who are perfectionists. Another letter from Laurence Olivier:

2nd Aug. 1951

Dear Mr. Peake—(may I call you Mervyn),

To let you know that 'The Wit to Woo' is not being idled about with. I want you to know that it is being read now by Tennant; I think you should also know that it is on the cards that you are to be a party to the shattering, ear-splitting, smashing up of one of those great old theatrical partnerships.

Vivien seems to like the play more than I don't like it, and so there is nothing to do but to offer it round to other producers than myself—producers of her choosing. Therefore, unless you have wishes to the contrary, as soon as Tennant has read it, it will go to Peter Brook, who is the first producer of her choice; from then on round, if necessary.

I hope you have another copy, so that we can keep this one for this purpose.

Yours, with a stiff upper lip—

Larry.

I suppose we had both become used to the world of waiting, of no decisions, of being postponed. I don't like the world of the theatre behind the scenes. There are too many people involved, too many vested interests. I prefer the solitary world of a poem, or a room in which to paint, and when you have painted what you are trying to achieve then comes the time when you have to try to sell it. Only then things become ugly.

★   ★   ★

The play was one among many things. It strikes me as inconceivable that one man could do so many things so well, at the same time, as did Mervyn. The play was being written, he had been asked by Eyre and Spottiswoode to write a long short story to be included in an anthology of three stories by John Wyndham, William Golding and Mervyn Peake, entitled *Sometime Never*, and which won a science fiction award some time later in America. It was called *Boy in Darkness* and was Titus outside the *Titus* books.

He was illustrating *Alice in Wonderland* for a Swedish publisher, producing poems, paintings, teaching painting twice a week, and beginning *Titus Alone*, the third and what was the last book of what was called a trilogy, but which would never have ended then if nature had in her aggressive way not taken possession of all that made him a unique person.

Later, *Titus Alone* will be explained, but already there were plans for a fourth book. Nothing so tidy as a trilogy had been envisaged.

Titus among the

Snows	Fires	Affluence
Mountains	Floods	Debt
Islands	Typhoons	Society
Rivers	Doldrums	
Archipelagos	Famines	
Forests	Pestilences	
Lagoons	Poverty	

Soldiers	Monsters	Pirates
Thieves	Hypocrites	Mermaids
Actors	Madmen	Dreamers
Painters	Bankers	Decadents
Psychiatrists	Angels	Athletes
Labourers	Devils	Invalids
Eccentrics	Mendicants	Blood-Sportsmen
Lepers	Vagrants	
Lotus Eaters		
Shapes	Sounds	Colours
Echoes	Tones	Scents
Textures		

What a book it would have been.

★   ★   ★

The dreams and ideas of *Titus 4* were far away. The dreams of *Titus Alone* were taking shape, with immense difficulty, unlike the preceding two, *Titus Groan* and *Gormenghast*, which must have torn his imagination apart but not his physical being.

It seemed that our holiday in Spain had assuaged the tremors, had calmed the troubled mind. So full of hope are human beings that we were becalmed for a short spell, before life took over again.

It is hard to write of someone else's pain dispassionately. But to watch degeneration, the slow degeneration, both mental and physical, of a brain and of a being is perhaps more painful than the sudden shock of assassination or instant death. If I had to choose the death of someone I loved, if it had to be brutal I would say let it be sudden, don't let it linger until what you are seeing, or whom you are seeing, bears no resemblance to the being you knew.

From now on, it is no use pretending that life had not

changed course. Difficult to say how, but the need for financial success seemed to grow deeper and more urgent. One thing which happened during a summer holiday assuaged some of this urgency.

Mervyn was offered an exhibition in Dublin. He went over to Ireland and stayed with friends in Galway, then wrote to say that he had done a great batch of line drawings which 'are going to be shown to local aesthetes—or rather, horsey Irish women who are very rich and buy signatures—Sickert, John, Innes, etc.'.

In another letter from Ireland he wrote trying to put his ideas of writing and painting into some kind of intellectual order:

(1) To canalize my chaos. To pour it out through the gutters of Gormenghast. To make not only tremendous stories in paint that approximate to the visual images in Gormenghast, but to create arabesques, abstracts, of thrilling colour, worlds on their own, landscapes and roofscapes and skyscrapes peopled with hierophants and lords—the fantastic and the grotesque, and to use paint as though it were meat and drink.

To restore to painting the giant groupings of the old masters—Tintoretto, Goya, Velasquez.

To make studies and cartoons for each canvas. To find myself by ploughing headlong into a genre, and by so doing to evolve a way of painting ANYTHING, from an angel to an apple.

To incorporate within the canvases, that in themselves would be masterly and original, still-lifes, or boys or buildings, and skies based on perception.

He needed three concurrent lives to do all that was simmering, later to boil over, in his restless brain, and his imagination which could find no rest.

I am too rich already, for my eyes
Mint gold, while my heart cries
'O cease!
Is there no rest from richness, and no peace
For me again?'
For gold is pain,
And the edged coins can smart,
And beauty's metal weighs upon the heart.

How can I spend this coinage when it floods
So ceaselessly between the lids,
And gluts my vaults with bright
Shillings of sharp delight
Whose every penny is coloured money?

Storm, harvest, flood or snow
Over the generous country as I go
And gather helplessly,
New wealth from all I see
In every spendthrift thing—
O then I long to spring
Through the charged air, a wastrel, with not one
Farthing to weigh me down,
But hollow! foot to crown
To prance immune among vast alchemies,
To prance! and laugh! my heart and throat and eyes
Emptied of all
Their golden gall.

*   *   *

The exhibition opened in Dublin, and I had letters about it,
but little mention of any financial benefit. The date and time of
his return was fixed. It was to be a night flight, so that his return to Wallington would be in the early hours of the morning.

I had gone to bed, knowing and longing for his return.

When one is suddenly awakened at night, there is always a sense of unreality, so that in the morning it is difficult to know if what has happened is dream or actuality.

This night I was awakened, the light by the bed, and the slow lids lifting, to see Mervyn standing there. He asked me to close my eyes which had, with so much difficulty, only a second ago opened. It was a simple concession. I closed them, and heard a crackling sound, the sound that crisp paper makes, together with a shuffling sound of someone moving quietly. It seemed to continue endlessly, but in that state of half-awareness it was an infinity of sound until I was asked to re-open my eyes.

They were dulled by sleep but they opened, and were only with difficulty able to grasp what they thought they saw. It looked as though the bed was covered with white waves, an endless sea of paper, which when I sat up undulated slowly like gentle froth. What I saw is still like a dream. The bed *was* covered with white waves, a sea of £5 notes. The crisp white notes, which gave one a feeling of enormous affluence, covered the bed. Surely no other paper money has ever had such magic. Money from the sale of drawings in Dublin. Is it sad that it gave me a sense of relief, when I think back to the heart-burn that the first sale of a drawing gave me? I think it is sad, but now we had three children, and three months' holiday from teaching at the Central School of Art with no money coming in.

It is difficult to remember how many £5 notes there were, but there seemed to be enough to get through those arid months ahead. We put them in a drawer, and there was a feeling of benediction in their whiteness and crispness.

It was almost possible to understand a little the feelings of a miser, except that this money was for using.

*   *   *

We played tennis of a kind, in the garden, and quoits, and cricket with the boys and some of their friends. We went to swimming pools. I painted, and was to have an exhibition in the autumn. *The Wit to Woo* had been finally dropped by the Oliviers.

Ziegfield Theatre,
New York.

My dear Mervyn,

Thank you so much for your delightful letter of the 9thish ultish.

I am afraid our ideas regarding 'The Wit to Woo' came to a natural standstill when the only three producers that we could see handling the job well, reluctantly turned it down all one after another, and the answer to your question as to how things stand. . . . 'Still', is the rather brutal, but simple one.

I am awfully sad about this. We have tried to get the thing going, but Vivien I know would not consider doing it under any other direction than that which we have already sought in vain.

Our time in New York has been intense in every conceivable way.

We look forward so much to seeing you later in the year.

Ever,
Larry O.

It had been sent to Anthony Quayle, who wrote from the Stratford-on-Avon Memorial Theatre:

January 14th 1952.

My dear Mervyn,

I am very sorry not to have written before and humbly apologize. I have now read 'The Wit to Woo' twice, and find it absolutely fascinating. I am sure it could be a very big success. I think that Vivien would be quite excellent in it, and I think that Michael Redgrave would be wonderful as Percy Trellis. Please let us keep in touch with it. I would really love to produce it—if I were a manager I would love to buy it. Unfortunately, I cannot give you any clear idea of when I shall be free. At the moment my horizon seems to be cluttered with a lot of plans—none of which may materialize. But please remember that I should be very thrilled to produce the play for you if you need a producer.

Should Vivien wish to forgo her option on it I think I could probably find a way to another very good management putting it on, though that again is a bit conjectural. Anyhow, let me hear from you. I would love to know how things develop.

Best wishes—
Tony.

*   *   *

There were other things happening, though, to lessen the disappointments which seemed to be endless with his play.

Commercial television had started around this time, and Mervyn went with an idea to the head of the children's programmes of A.T.V. A book which he had written and illustrated called *Letters from a Lost Uncle*, published after the end of the war, seemed almost a 'natural' to be adapted.

This time, the answer was yes, and a fairly quick yes. Renewed hope and vigour accompanied the affirmative.

It was to be a series of twelve programmes. Mervyn was to do the drawings from the original, mainly wash and heavy line, over which the camera would play, and the text would be spoken by an actor as the camera moved over the pictures. It was a weekly serial, and he had to do at least twelve very large

'Head floats about me . . .', 1957

Drawings in Madrid
1956

drawings each week, and take them up to the television studio in time for rehearsal. Once, having arrived at Victoria with his large portfolio, when he was already on the bus towards the studio he found he had left them in the train. He jumped off the bus, and rushed back to the station. In a whirl and a panic he made for the lost property office. A week's work! There was no sign of them, nothing and nobody could help. He had to return home, phone the studios, explain what had happened, and stay up night and day until he had worked all over again on the same drawings.

Financially, it was probably the largest amount of money that he had received, but we were still badly in debt from the house in Kent, so that half of everything which came in went directly to help pay off our stupidity in becoming certainly 'landed' but perhaps not gentry.

The programme was apparently highly rated in opinion polls, but it didn't lead to anything further, which, considering the strain of the work, was perhaps a good thing.

*   *   *

One evening, Mervyn received a phone call from a man whom he knew only slightly. A group of his friends, who were all specialists in one way or another, had decided to make up a group to go to Yugoslavia. They wanted Mervyn to go as an artist—the others were an archaeologist, a historian, a geologist, a naturalist, a photographer, a writer (though Mervyn could have done for that too). They planned to do a television programme seen through all these different eyes. It was an original idea, and he decided to go. The term of teaching was over. I think the trip was partly sponsored, or helped financially in some way, otherwise it would not have been possible for him to have gone. The only essential articles for travelling were materials for working with. No oils, but an infinite supply of paper, water-colours, pens and pencils, *conte*, quick and sudden for the quick and sudden sight or thought. Apart from these it was very rudimentary, almost elementary in that it was suggested that essentials at that time to be taken to Yugoslavia were soap and lavatory paper.

It was an exciting prospect, to be going to a completely unknown country with people of such diverse talents and with very little knowledge of what lay in store. Alas, what letters I received have been lost, but I can remember some incidents which were related to me on the return home. I have also a batch of drawings done under conditions of varying degrees of difficulty. A handsome, magnificent old man, bearded and long-haired, a prophet, threatened Mervyn with a knife, on seeing himself being drawn. Both escaped with their lives, and Mervyn with his drawings. Nuns on a boat, sailing down the Adriatic; peasants, who gave him and one other member of the group the kind of hospitality that meant that they themselves might go without for weeks to come, generosity akin to madness, and the lack of linguistic communication stultifying all means of gratitude, except by gesture and sign.

The articles already mentioned as being essential equipment certainly proved to be so. There was one story, which is funny, I think. Approaching the end of the journey, it was decided to spend a night in the best hotel in Zagreb. No one had had a bath for the past three weeks, and the need for one had become a matter of some necessity.

Mervyn found a bathroom, and filled the bath with hot water, having remembered to put in the plug. He lay in the blissful warmth, dreaming dreams, his clothing arbitrarily discarded around the floor. With his toe he unhooked the plug, after an hour of meditation, and lay with closed eyes whilst the water gently seeped away. It was after a little time that he opened his eyes, and saw to his astonishment his clothes floating like ship-wrecked mariners around him. The bathroom had many facilities, but *not* one for disposing of the water. He went into the passage in a towel, and met a friendly house-maid. By gesture he took her to the bathroom to disclose the damage. Her reaction was one of immediate laughter, and shaking of head and hand, as if to a child who has misbehaved but with whom one is not irredeemably angry. I'm not quite sure of the sequel.

There was little to buy in Yugoslavia at that time, but a bottle of Slivovitz was brought back, and a doll in national costume for our daughter, which began a great collection of dolls in national dress.

As is the way with many projects, the visit to Yugoslavia did not materialize as had been envisaged. It was a pity, because the idea had been so good, to see one place through so many different eyes and minds. There was a small television programme, but on a very minor scale. Mervyn was interviewed on children's television, and several of his drawings shown, but the main idea had been jettisoned.

*   *   *

So once more there was a return to the struggle.

Mervyn sent *The Wit to Woo* to John Clements, with his wife Kay Hammond in mind to play the only woman's part in it. They were very intrigued by it, and a good deal of correspondence passed and hope revived once more.

If the play had been the only project at this time, we both might have given up hope in every direction, but now, looking through all the ideas, projects, and actual finished achievements, I am overwhelmed by the proliferation.

Mervyn had begun on the third book of the *Titus Groan* series, as yet untitled, and during the Christmas holidays in 1954 he went to stay at a pub in Dedham to enable him to write with less disturbance than he would have had at home. The tremors in his hands had returned. They were still only slight, but enough to make writing, which he always did in long-hand, more tiring. He found concentration more difficult, and returned home having written with far more difficulty than he had in the first two books.

He had been commissioned by the Swedish Radio, who published books in English, to illustrate *The Adventures of Tom Thumb*, and a year later, *The Further Adventures of Tom Thumb*. They were published very attractively in miniature form, which is perhaps appropriate to the subject.

From all the activity and the amount of work done, our finances should not have been in the parlous state which seemed to be habitual. We were still paying for our lost sojourn in Kent, and apart from that book illustration could scarcely be called lucrative, particularly when practised by someone who was a perfectionist, and not easily satisfied with his own work. I did a few book jackets, which, if one's livelihood depended on them, would provide very few luxuries in life.

I was painting every day, in two attics at the top of the house, where my cats followed and sat on the piles of paper which littered every working room. I exhibited in the London Group, in the Woman's International, and in various other mixed exhibitions; and I was working for a one-man show later that year.

I always seem to have been able to paint when there is intense life surrounding me, despite the eternal meals, the fights of one's children, and the constant demands of domesticity.

It is now, with more time and less friction, that I find it harder. I miss Mervyn. He was a fair critic, and honest. Sometimes, I hated what he said, and would fight against it, but knew that he nearly always probed to the essential heart of a painting or a drawing.

In those attic rooms, the surrounding suburb disappeared, and I entered the world of my own making, and the familiar smell of turpentine. My painting was changing and had changed a great deal since the early days of my marriage, when it was unrestrainedly romantic, as I was myself. I certainly knew a great deal more technically, and began to use different materials and to experiment with shapes and colours, but I have never been able to divorce myself aesthetically, to decide between life and painting. My mainspring has always been the heart and not the head, but with more knowledge the heart can be controlled.

I painted a great deal from my children—using their play and their turmoil, boys on stilts, handstands, somersaulting, dressed up in Indian war-dress, trying to achieve the rhythm of their movements in simplified form.

★   ★   ★

It seems incredible that we were able to part-exchange our Wolseley Hornet car, which had by now very little left inside to make it a going concern, for a wooden shooting-brake which to our children was a revelation of beauty, even after the mushrooms started growing on the inside of the roof.

We went for picnics to the country and sea, and Mervyn, Clare, and I slept in it, with the boys in a tent outside. I never could equate the driving of a car with Mervyn, but for all the excitement and wrong turnings, we saw a good deal more of England than we should have done if he or I had been more of a map reader.

Our garden in Wallington was very large, too large for us to dig and delve ourselves. By some means we found a man who was willing to work in it for six months in exchange for our shooting-brake, which had proved more expensive than we had imagined it would. We knew or thought we knew his

name, but not his address—but it seemed unimportant. At the
end of the six months he claimed our 'dreamland', as Fabian
had called the car, which was as it should be, as both sides had
agreed in writing to this rather strange form of payment. What
we had not agreed was that all our garden tools should also be
included. We found an empty shed, but never again heard of
our gardener or his car.

*   *   *

Not having heard about the play for some time, Mervyn
must have written to John Clements, for he wrote in reply:

My dear Mervyn

. . . I gave the play to Robert Hamer, who, as you
probably know, is one of the really top film directors in this
country. He directed among other things 'Kind Hearts and
Coronets'.

. . . He is wildly enthusiastic about 'The Wit to Woo',
but says he couldn't do it as his next one because there is too
little time to prepare it for film purposes. But it is something
that he and I would very much like to discuss with you for a
future date if it interests you. The delay in writing to you
about it has been that Hamer was a long time over
it—insisted that he wouldn't be rushed in savouring writing
of such quality—and so on. . . .

Yours,
John.

Perhaps we both had now begun to realize that disappointments and setbacks in the world of the theatre were almost
more relentless than in the world of painting and writing,
although we both had experienced the normal lot of artists or
writers in the heart-burning rejections and, perhaps even
worse, indifference.

Alice in Wonderland, which Mervyn had been originally commissioned to illustrate by a Swedish publisher in 1946, had been accepted by Alan Wingate, in England, and came out in 1954. Naturally, there was a reserve on many people's parts to accept illustrations other than Tenniel's, but the drawings were well reviewed on the whole.

A letter came from Graham Greene in response to the book:

10th Sept., 1954.

Dear Mervyn,

How very kind of you indeed to send me Alice's Adventures in Wonderland. I have always liked your illustrations for this enormously. You are the first person who has been able to illustrate the book satisfactorily since Tenniel, though I still argue as I think I argued with you years ago that your Alice is a little bit too much of a gamin. But here they seem to have eliminated her nearly altogether. I look in vain at first glance for a full length of her. I do wish they had given you better paper.

Yours,
Graham.

Yet another book came out with drawings, called *Figures of Speech*, published by Gollancz. It is as the title indicates. There is no text, and it was intended for moments of light-heartedness when people could guess at the figures of speech upon which the drawings played. I think they are very funny, but to some people they are facetiously so. As far as I can remember this book was also remaindered. Not a new experience, but always one that hurts anew, and perhaps hurts the publishers even more in a different way.

★   ★   ★

We had a friend living with us at this time, named Aaron Judah, who had a room at the top of the house, which he fitted up with gadgets of Heath Robinson ingenuity. He had the room nominally, in exchange for sitting in, when needed, and sometimes fetching Clare from school, if I had been in town and couldn't get back in time.

He was a writer, and just then had an idea for a play which he had worked out, and wished to collaborate in, with Mervyn writing and he supplying the technical workings. I must admit that I was not sanguine at the prospect of the disappointments ahead, but the theatre attracted Mervyn greatly, and he was also interested in the theme, which perhaps had its genesis in *Oblomov*. He had always been fascinated by the one or two individuals of great talent whom he had known who had nevertheless decided against using their natural gifts, whether through indolence or cynicism, and devoted their lives to nothingness on a grand scale. This was roughly the theme of *Mr Loftus*, or its alternative title *And a House of Air*.

So began another marathon of patience. The play was written, far more quickly than was *The Wit to Woo*, and it started on its rounds. Its life, rather like its theme, has been lazy.

One of the first people to whom it was sent for a reaction was Kenneth Tynan:

Dear Mr. Peake,

I apologise for my delays in reading and returning 'Mr. Loftus'. I can see in it some fine pointed writing, and a lot of quite unforced pathos, plus a lovely part for a bravura actor to sink his teeth into. What slightly worries me is what might be called a foothold in reality. Your characters weave some splendid verbal wreathes for themselves, but seem to be figures in a pageant rather than people in a play. Also I found the motivation a bit obscure at times: I wasn't quite clear why Flora left Loftus: but perhaps this was due to hasty reading. On the whole while I admire your verbal virtuosity enormously, 'Loftus' isn't really my kind of play. I hope you'll go ahead, get it produced, and prove me wrong. And let's meet again soon, when I get back from Moscow.

Yours,

Kenneth Tynan.

★   ★   ★

Titus Alone had begun, to a slow start. It was perhaps more difficult to be outside the world which had been created as a world within a world than to be in a world which was probably closer to this one, and yet alien. There was too much—the world is too much with us. People have said that Mervyn lived in an ivory tower, or that his books are an escape from life. I think they are an extension, full of humour and compassion: the extremes that are so much a part of life, the quirks and the norms, and *Titus Alone* hints more by its veracity than many a book, factually correct.

There was still two days a week teaching life-drawing at the Central School of Art, which at least brought in bread and margarine. I think Mervyn enjoyed teaching, or, at least, trying to communicate what he felt was the essence of drawing. He had enormous sympathy with people on the edge, as students are.

He was able to use the lithography room at the Central, and experimented in the medium, which excited him very much. He had been commissioned to illustrate *Bleak House*, and did several lithographs, poor Jo, Skimpole, Lady Dashwood, etc. A very evocative set of drawings was produced, only for it to be discovered that the publisher who had commissioned them had disintegrated, so that no book was forthcoming. It is impossible to imagine anything so straightforward as a book being published without complication, but still less so that a play can be written, and within a certain time limit, produced.

Another letter came from John Clements about *The Wit to Woo*:

My dear Mervyn,

I am delighted to have a script of 'The Wit to Woo' always at my elbow.

Katie and I are still desperately anxious to do it in the theatre, and one of these days—if of course we are not forestalled, I am determined to bring that about.

So don't for Heavens sake let anyone else have it without giving us a snap refusal!

In the near future my whole organization is to undergo many changes and when they happen it may make it much more possible for me to come to you with a definite proposition. The making of a TV film would not in any way affect that.

In fact in my view it might easily enhance its chances in the theatre rather than the reverse.

My best wishes to you both from both of us—

Yours,
John.

How could one help but feel a certain hope? Why did Mervyn place so much in it, when his own media had not in themselves brought respite from worry? Up to a certain age, it may be right and proper for a writer or a painter to struggle, not only for recognition but for a certain financial easing, but after forty a man should be able to work without the constant strain that damages the mainspring. There is no one to blame, but perhaps ourselves, in that money had never been the reason for doing anything. But this play was one thing where

Mervyn saw likelihood of the kind of financial reward that he had never envisaged with drawing or painting or poetry. It was becoming an ogre, equating success with money. And yet Mervyn often told me of Cézanne who, after he had been painting a portrait over a period of years and was asked how he felt about it, replied, 'I am not displeased with the left elbow.' Cézanne, I think, was not too financially embarrassed, but to both of us it was a wonderful disdain for the world. Only the world was creeping in.

* * *

I have no letter, but somewhere the Clements had to drop their option on the play. I know they wished to do it, but the theatre must be harsher even than the Bond Street galleries. It really was *not* our world, but the dreadful devil was beating Mervyn, and he must have sent it to Peter Hall at the Arts Theatre, from whom he received this reply:

The Arts Theatre   26th March, 1955.

Dear Mr. Peake,

Herewith your script of 'The Wit to Woo'. I have had no chance to read it with any close attention, but I skimmed through it last night, and I must say I found it wonderful. So, please, if the Clements don't want to do it, may I have the script back so that we can consider doing it here?

In any case I would very much like to have a long talk about 'And a House of Air' (Mr. Loftus). I think your plays have the most enormous possibilities and I would very much like to do one of them.

Perhaps you would let me know when you come back to England.

With best wishes for your trip.

Yours sincerely,
Peter Hall.

Disillusion never set in on Mervyn's side, although I had far more reservations now with anything to do with the theatre. For me, the silent worlds of painting and writing had an intrinsic truth, whatever happened once they had left their birthplace.

I think it was the only thing I could not share with completely in the making. I was becoming afraid of what was happening to Mervyn. He was becoming more ill. The tremors in his hands and in his legs were more pronounced. He tired too easily. What used to be easy became more difficult. The theatre remained the promised land which he longed for, in some way he felt to prove himself, as a man who could make money, to give presents to his family. The dreadful power of money: it is demoralizing without enough, demoralizing with too much.

*   *   *

Our eldest son had become greatly interested in drumming, and through holding jobs, and newspaper rounds, had bought himself a drum-set. He had friends who played other instruments, so that in the evenings the house rocked to the sounds of a group. It even reached the attic where I painted—Titus was not so Alone as he might have wished to be.

Titus Alone was growing more impatient to be written, and one holiday Mervyn went over to Sark to try to find the serenity which he now craved. I had letters from him telling me of the progress.

. . . the weather bleaches my soul. It's like a furnace, but I am thriving on it, and am writing at top gear. THANK YOU sweet one. What you say about Titus 3 helps me. Titus 3 is for you as they are all for you. . . . My brain is clearing day by day. With a strong healthy brain one can make studies—and when you have more time from chores and less fatigue we will make progress together.

God bless my darling—you are deep in my heart.

★   ★   ★

He must have had to return from Sark, which had always, since his very early days, held something especial for him, but whilst he was there this time the B.B.C. were broadcasting an adaptation of his book *Mr Pye*, which was set on the island.

I went to the rehearsals, and saw at first hand the production of a play. The music had been written by Malcolm Arnold, and the characters coming alive, in front of so cold a thing as a microphone, was a minor revelation. Mervyn didn't hear the play, but the rest of us listened in our various ways, and apart from the barriers I was developing against the theatre I found it rather wonderful to hear and even to see, through sound, the characters alive, the people he had created, that one knew.

A year earlier *Titus Groan* had been adapted for the Third Programme. Mervyn had done the adaptation, which was a formidable task, as a book of 200,000 words had to be condensed into one hour's listening. It should not have been condensed so drastically. But even so, the actors became the characters and it seemed as though the world of Gormenghast had found itself, living here and now—the people that we knew, just speaking, more real than any politician with his platitudes.

A book called *More Prayers and Graces* was published by Gollancz in 1957. It was a follow-on to an earlier book called *Prayers and Graces*, which seems to have had the biggest sales of any book that Mervyn had done drawings for. There had been an outright payment, so there were no royalties. Likewise with the second book, so although both books sold well, probably better than most that Mervyn had illustrated, that was financially all there was.

*   *   *

Whatever happened to *The Wit to Woo* after Peter Hall's letter I have neither recollection nor letters, until one came:

Jan. 8th 1957.

Dear Mr. Peake,

I have read these plays once; which is not enough. But enough to find them intriguing, disturbing and exciting.

Will you please give me more time to read them again, get 'others' to do so, and then let you know what can be done.

Kind regards,

Yours sincerely,

Michael Codron.

This was no longer enthusiasm without prospect. Through Mervyn's agent it became not just enthusiasm, but a concrete proposal. Contracts were signed, and the paraphernalia of the theatre slowly creaked into motion. Michael Codron was a young producer, and he intended to put it on at the Arts Theatre in London, with Peter Wood directing.

It was hardly credible. The play had been begun seven years ago, and had already lived a life that few people could hope for themselves. The illustrious of the theatre had toyed with it, and rejected it, but somebody loved it, and its seven years gestation was at last in labour.

The cast was chosen, and after that rehearsals began. Mervyn went to as many as he could, and often came home late, excited and expectant, full of regeneration. It is a pity that he didn't design the sets himself, but I suppose he would not have had the time to do so with the multifarious work in other directions.

It was exciting for him, like the dumb suddenly being able to speak. To hear his words which he had known for so long being heard, and in most cases, given the meaning that he had strived for.

We both went up to the Arts Theatre and I met the cast. Certainly, they all seemed enthusiastic, and how could one fail to like them after so many years of waiting?

We went to the dress rehearsal, and it was touching for me, as I had not seen or heard it on stage before, to hear words that I had known so long being spoken with the wit and understanding with which they had been engendered, although many critics were later to disagree with that.

The first night was 12 March 1957, and through the imaginative generosity of an old friend, Laura Beckingsale, who had been present at Mervyn's birth forty-six years ago in China, we spent the night at the Royal Court Hotel in Sloane Square. We had had experience of private views, and of books being published, but never of such a soul-baring experience as a play, where you can see and hear and be infiltrated by the comment and the mood.

I had a dinner jacket made for Mervyn as a present, and we both took some form of tranquillizers. Neither of us could help the other, except by the negative things that one always says at moments of stress. Once at the Arts Theatre it seemed less momentous, as there were many friends to give the sense that we were not entirely alone in the world. John Clements and Kay Hammond were there, which seemed to both of us a generous gesture.

The theatre was full, and it appeared as though the years of waiting might be rewarded. It was a silly thought, as the audience had in it so many people who would like it to be a success.

Nevertheless, there was a reception for it which seemed to give point to the waiting. People had laughed, had been amused; and not, I think, only because they were friends and relations. It would take an even smaller theatre than the Arts to fill it with partisans.

Having seen the actors afterwards, and all the excitement which first nights carry, we had a feeling that something was going right.

We were taken out for a sumptuous dinner by relations, at Pruniers, and never has lobster tasted so sweet. A return to the hotel, and a deep sleep, to awaken to the almost outworn cliché of the morning reviews.

They were neither good nor bad, but mostly condescending and ungenerous. How easily and quickly can a man be disposed of!

*   *   *

We packed our bags, but did not run. We returned to Wallington, and from this awful date life has changed.

It cannot be laid at any door, but disappointment, built up by hope for too long, can damage a brain already too prolific.

Mervyn went to bed when we got home, and became delirious. It was as though everything that he had been holding on to had disintegrated. I sent for the doctor who gave him tranquillizers, but who was unable to diagnose any physical trouble.

For the next few days he languished, and the symptoms of tremors in hands and legs became more and more manifest.

One day his memory went completely, and he had hallucinations. My two sons took my daughter out all day, and I phoned a doctor in London who came down to see Mervyn.

He diagnosed a complete breakdown, and made an appointment with a neurologist for the following day.

Somehow or other we must have got up to London to the

hospital, and it was decided that he should go immediately to a hospital and have treatment. Even at that time, I felt it was a physical illness—what is known as Parkinson's Disease, because I had seen an old friend with almost identical symptoms—although there seemed also to be every reason for a mental breakdown. The play was forgotten, the reviews which came in were now a matter of indifference. A friend drove Mervyn and me to Virginia Water Hospital, where he was admitted, and I had to sign forms to allow him to be given electrical treatment. I had never seen male nurses before. I had never seen mad people before. How incredibly worse it must have been for Mervyn. His first letter to me said:

> I have almost lost my identity—I long for your white arms around my neck. I am afraid of something subtle. It is the smell of the place—its miles and miles of corridors—the expression on the faces—some of whom have been here for years.
>
> I will never write about mad people again—I am in a kind of dream—or nightmare, and I yearn for your touch.
>
> Maeve! Never! Never again! It has done something to me. I have played too much around the edge of madness—oh I could cry to be free.

I could write a book about an illness which robbed my husband of dignity, of coherent thought, of all his creative powers, and left him an emptiness of tragedy. We have all gone through the extremes of bitterness in watching a citadel fall by slow and tortuous degrees, but even now, at this time, there was still a little left of the life which we had shared.

★   ★   ★

It was an arduous time. I had the three children, and two or three times a week I went to Virginia Water, after taking my daughter to school and making arrangements for her to be collected in the afternoon. Mervyn was being given electrical treatment, which he feared as a child fears darkness. He would ring me two or three times a day begging me to fetch him home.

I thought that the treatment he was receiving was for his good, so I had to try to calm him and tell him that what was being done was for his good. It was as heart-rending as leaving one's child with strangers.

He did write some poems, and also painted and drew whilst he was there:

> Out of the overlapping
> Leaves of my brain came tapping. . . .
> Tapping . . . a voice that is not mine alone:
> Nor can the woodpecker
> Claim it as his own: the flicker
> Deep in the foliage belongs to neither
> Birds, men or dreams.
>
> It is as far away as childhood seems.

Titus Alone was neglected, and the fate of *The Wit to Woo* had been decided. It ran for two or three weeks at the Arts Theatre, and came off with no further offers. In all, Mervyn received £17 for it.

*   *   *

As he seemed to progress he came home at weekends, and brought drawings he had done, poems he had written. Most of them have now been published, although at the time I sent them to various periodicals and they were rejected. Most of his poems then were nothing to do with his environment, which from his first letter to me had a nightmare quality, but were

Drawings in Madrid
1956

Drawings in Madrid
1956

lyrical and full of a nostalgic lost beauty. This is only one which seemed to come straight from what he was experiencing:

> Heads float about me; come and go, absorb me;
> Terrify me that they deny the nightmare
> That they should be, defy me;
> And all the secrecy; the horror
> Of truth, of this intrinsic truth
> Drifting, ah God, along the corridors
> Of the world; hearing the metal
> Clang; and the rolling wheels.
> Heads float about me haunted
> By solitary sorrows.

It is almost too painful for me to re-read his letters from this time. All, full of hope and projects, ideas for books and paintings, and through all a love which sustained the forebodings.

As he seemed to improve a little, he began to write *Titus Alone* again. It was not easy, as he had been having electrical treatment which affected the memory and made clear thinking impossible.

After about nine months of treatment for a nervous breakdown Mervyn was discharged from the hospital. It was indicated that there was nothing further they could do, as in fact he had the early symptoms of Parkinson's Disease.

The Central School of Art had kept his job open for him all this time, which was almost more than one could expect, but it alleviated one of the foremost worries which was, naturally, financial. We had never been able to straighten our finances since our foolish foray into Kent.

During this first time in hospital, there was unbelievable generosity from friends and relations. His brother, in a most wonderful letter, sent him £1,000 to help clear the overdraft. We couldn't believe it when we opened the envelope and saw such a sum. There was hope, and faith, and charity.

*   *   *

The summer holidays came, and we decided to go with the children to Sark. It did seem as though the dark days were over. It was a wonderful time. The island always seemed to have the effect of a magic wand. The miracles that one expected in childhood almost came to pass. This holiday had a healing quality. To climb down to bays, opulently curved and golden, where there was neither sight nor sound from other humans, except distant shapes and echoes of voices, was the peace and the excitement we all craved. Watching a school of porpoises, discovering caves which may well have hidden treasure trove. There are many bays in Sark, and each has a different mood. The grey stony bays, austere and cold, and the bays with rockpools in which our daughter sat, screaming with joy. Watching trawlers and fishing boats, hearing the sea-gulls, their voices harsh, and matching the shrillness of the child. Cormorants and puffins. Picnics and games, and crossness on the return home, because whichever bay one goes to there is a steep climb back to the top, and even the exhilaration of doing what one wants cannot always preclude the quarrels of children and their parents.

*   *   *

So the various terms started again, and we all went back to our own occupations. Mervyn once again started his teaching, and at the same time he was offered an exhibition of line drawings at the Waddington Galleries, who had now moved from Dublin to London. *Titus Alone* was progressing, but slowly.

How could one fail to notice the slowing down once more, both physically and mentally, and the hand, once so steady, unable to control pen or pencil with its former ease? It was lucky that he had a drawer full of line drawings which could be exhibited, as he could never have made any especially for it.

As the weeks progressed, so it was manifest that medical advice should again be sought. He was admitted to a neurological hospital to undergo tests of all kinds, and the private view of his exhibition took place during this sojourn, although he was allowed up to come to it. He sold several drawings, which at least was a boost to his morale, and I have just come across a very excellent review of the exhibition in a paper called *Freedom*, which is an anarchist newssheet. There must have been other reviews, but they are lost, and anarchy prevails.

One learns the big things in life sometimes in small ways. I had asked to see a doctor at the hospital, to know as far as anyone could know what lay ahead. I was told that the doctor attending him was busy, but if I would wait in the hall I could see him on his way out—almost as though I was about to ask him to tea, not as though I wished to know something which would affect all our lives.

A dreadful feeling of insignificance overcame me as I waited. Was it complete lack of imagination on the doctor's part that he told me the most devastating news that I could hear of my husband, standing in a hall, with the never-ending stream of people who pass and re-pass one almost somnambulistically in all hospitals?

He said, 'Your husband has premature senility.'

He was then forty-six years old.

*   *   *

He returned home with pills, and with perhaps a little hope, as he never knew the possibilities of his cruel disease.

Christmas came and went, and he had a sense of great urgency in completing *Titus Alone*. It was now impossible to write at home. We had heard that often writers, or anyone seeking peace, could go to Aylesford Priory, a monastery in Kent, and live and work there, without necessarily being a Catholic, or taking part in any of the religious services. So we fixed for him to go there, to try to write without the rigours of a family round him.

He was still able to work, but there was an appalling restlessness, night and day, which I was afraid would disturb the other guests, which later proved to be true.

I did have some letters from him:

My own Special beauty queen!

Today (and its only 5 p.m.) I have got on like a house on fire (9 pages) and I am going on this evening.

It is a beautiful 12th century Priory, set on a square with a big green in the centre. There is a library, but its full of religious books. There is also a 'trinket' shop, so I can get you and Clare something. There's not much to appeal to les garçons, but I'll try.

I've driven myself to work and I'll have something to show you. . . .

Am really enjoying and profiting by the break—Women are allowed too, if you wanted to come—it ain't half monastic. However I have a tame radiator. This really has been a great success thanks to you, dear one. I am writing well and steadily.

God Bless you all—I love you all, even the children.

Mervyn told me later that he had very controversial talks about painting and religion, and other aspects of life (if there are any), with the Prior.

I had a phone call one day, from the Priory, asking if I could fetch him home as he wasn't well and, as I had feared, was disturbing the other people. He couldn't sleep at nights, and was in the habit of pacing his room, and suffered quite obviously from loss of memory.

*　　　*　　　*

He came home to Wallington, but at least with *Titus Alone* almost completed. He wrote everything he ever did in long-hand, but on account of the tremors in his hand the writing had become almost incomprehensible. I think I was the only person who could decipher a great deal of what was written, so I decided to type it, with one finger. It's astonishing how quickly one can race along in so handicapped a fashion. I was able to refer to Mervyn when his writing became too difficult to understand.

It went to the publishers and was accepted in principle, although they felt at the time the writing was uneven—which, given the circumstances under which it was written, seemed a reasonable conclusion. It was as though Mervyn was no longer master of his own work. He wished to resist the deletions which were made, and some of which I agreed with, but his brain was no longer able to grope and, sickened as I was at the thought of anyone touching what he had done, it was, or seemed to be, a question of necessity.

Titus Alone was published in 1959, and received on the whole good reviews although it was naturally compared with its two predecessors, not unfavourably, but because it had entered a different world, more questioningly.

*　　　*　　　*

In the summer of 1959 a letter came from the B.B.C. Television Studios:

. . . I am wondering if it would perhaps be possible to do something on the programme 'Monitor', in connection with the forthcoming publication of 'Titus Alone'. We find it very difficult to handle novels as a rule, as one is usually discussing something quite unknown to the audience, and impossible to SHOW to them, in the sense that a picture or a piece of music can be shown. However, I remember seeing a few years ago some sketches you had done for 'Titus Groan' of Steerpike, Fuchsia, and I believe Swelter; and I had thought that if you had done, or could do similar sketches of 'Titus Alone' of some of the characters and situations, we might be able to organize a discussion around these. Alternatively, we might be able to expand the situation to take in the other sides of your work, as painter, illustrator, poet, etc.

As you can see, I'm thinking in a bit of a void at present. IF the idea appeals to you at all, I wonder if I could come down to Wallington some time for a couple of hours to discuss possibilities. . . .

I look forward to hearing your reactions.

David Jones.

It was a wonderful stimulus, but I felt almost certain that it would be beyond Mervyn. He had never wished to speak in public: his writing and painting had always spoken for him, but now his speech was beginning to slur and he could not think quickly. If he was asked a direct question about his work his thoughts could not assemble themselves.

A very nice young man came and spent several hours with us in Wallington, discussing the various ways in which the programme could be envisaged. I think he understood that Mervyn himself would be unable to speak, which was the integral part of the idea.

We received a letter a few days later:

. . . I have discussed the idea of filming at your house and studio with Peter Newington who produces 'Monitor'. He likes the idea in principle, but feels we must see how the sound recordings turn out before we make a final decision to go ahead with the story. We've found in the past that the success of a story like this depends entirely on how much you yourself can tell us about your work, and your attitudes to painting, writing etc., by way of commentary. To describe your work at second hand through the words of a narrator immediately lessens the impact and makes the thing less truthful, and where possible we try to avoid this. I'm sure, however, that we should be able to get some good material if I come down with a tape-recorder beforehand, and we really take our time over it. . . .

★   ★   ★

It would have been an impossible task to make the programme, and this was the case.

How Mervyn continued to be able to teach is a minor miracle. He had the journey to London, and then to the Central School from Victoria Station. I've always been very grateful to Morris Kesselman, who was head of the drawing department, for keeping him on when it seemed that he was no longer able to impart very much knowledge to his students.

We were wanting to leave Wallington for many reasons, not the least being the exhaustion he felt in making the journey to London twice a week. Our house was a Victorian Gothic white elephant, and for it we had been offered £1,000 five years previously. It was now more valuable, with the land, for redevelopment. We were offered a price which to us was unheard of, £8,000. We had never envisaged money in those terms. It meant that we could look for a house in London with real and not pretend money.

We looked at one house in Chelsea which even for us was too dilapidated, and then only at one other, which seemed right in every way. A small garden for cats to bask in with a walnut tree, which in London is rare, and a huge bay tree in the front, big enough to enrich the stews of all our friends for years to come.

★　　　★　　　★

It was almost like a release from prison to leave Wallington, despite the spaciousness of house and garden. I cannot say that any of our houses have been graciously appointed. They would not pass a good taste test, if only because the furniture has not been renewed, but the books and the paintings which I think of as the only things that I could not bear to be without were ever changing.

Everything seemed to go fairly easily, except that we nearly lost the house on account of neglecting to sign a document, but our neglect did not have too devastating an effect. We were able to make arrangements to move. We left quite an amount of antiquated sofas and chairs in the house, and we were told later that tramps made it their rendezvous until prised out by authority.

We had no regrets, and I know that our sons certainly had none; only my daughter, who had many friends, was apprehensive of London, the unknown.

I was preparing for an exhibition at the Woodstock Gallery, just off Bond Street. The upheaval of a move didn't help one's creative powers, although I had been painting until the time of the move, and I had most of the pictures ready.

We moved with our three cats and two children. The two eldest were no longer children. Sebastian had left home to work his way around Scandinavia, which in itself, from what he has recounted, could make an adventure story. Fabian was

at the Chelsea School of Art. Clare was still at school in
Wallington, and came home for weekends.

The cats went under the bath, and didn't reappear until the
hurly-burly of trudging feet subsided in the evening, and they
emerged to seek food and drink in unfamiliar places.

*   *   *

The house assembled itself fairly quickly. The same familiar
objects. It was as though we were for ever talking to ourselves.
The three vertebrae of a whale, which had been washed ashore
twenty or more years ago in Sark, were three of the most
important pieces of furnishing. The whale was dead, and
Mervyn had found it lying, how sadly so, in one of the bays.
He removed three of the vertebrae, and some of the ribs,
which he left in a cave to be cleansed for a year. The ribs were
too awkward to carry to England, but the vertebrae—then
whitened by the sun—were more easily transported. He wrote
a long narrative poem called 'A Reverie of Bone'. Some of the
lines in it were perhaps engendered by this whale, though
changed in form to a steed.

> . . . I ponder
> On sun-lit spires and in my reverie find
> The arc-ribbed courser, and his mount to be
> Whiter than sexless lilies and how slender
>
> The spleenful hands can turn:
>
> O ribs of light! Bright flight, yours are such stairs
> As wail at midnight when the sand meanders
> Through your cold rings that sieve the desert gale.

Never far from poetry, and yet growing away from it. Of
every form of human expression, poetry moved Mervyn

more than any other. He read it so beautifully, too. His voice was gentle, and he often read it aloud. He could quote, before his illness, poems from all periods. Love poems, funny poems, and the hymns of his childhood, as with the poems ancient and modern.

*   *   *

The private view of my exhibition came, and a few pictures were sold. A little time later I was offered a job as 'artist in residence' at a University in Indiana. Even if I had wished to take it, it would have been impossible to leave Mervyn, and I couldn't have done so.

In 1960 he had been commissioned by the Folio Society to illustrate Balzac's *Droll Stories*. We were both apprehensive as to whether he would be able to control his tremors, but he accepted the commission as we needed the money.

It was the first book that he had illustrated where he could not even read the text. He could read, but no longer fully comprehend what he saw on the page. I read all the stories for him, and chose the passages which I felt he would be able to see in his own idiosyncratic way.

It was a kind of nightmare. I was with him each day as he floundered, trying to draw what would have been second nature to him, a gift for his humour and his power of insight into another writer's mind, although illustration has often been belittled, particularly now. If he was at one with the author, it was not only interpretative but creative.

Somehow or other the drawings were achieved, with brush and water colour. Three colours were used, and I think the Folio Society was satisfied with them. At any rate they produced a book of great attraction.

Life had become almost impossible. His tremors precluded most normal activities. His walking was nearly non-existent, although he still dragged himself to the art school, and the nights were such that one could no longer envisage sleeping.

A school friend of mine, whose husband had Parkinson's Disease, told me of an operation that her husband had had, and to whom the benefits were immense.

It was obvious that life could not go on as it was. I wanted a miracle.

I went to see my doctor to ask him if he approved of the operation. In theory he did, but it seemed that there was not enough knowledge of the after-effects. The brain, and this particular brain. An undiscovered world, even in this scientific age.

Mervyn was ill with despair, and a longing for someone to piece him together again. I spoke to him of the operation, and to him it seemed like manna. We do clutch at straws. We went to see the neurological surgeon, who agreed that an operation could be beneficial. That the tremors and the malaise should be eased but, I think, we were given no assurances of complete success. It was left to me to make the decision. I decided that things could not be worse than they were (how little I knew), and arrangements were made for him to go into the hospital as a private patient. National health meant a long delay, and the money from Balzac's *Droll Stories* paid for the fees and the room.

Whilst the operation was in progress his brother was with me, and of all strange things we went to a cinema in Victoria and saw a film called *Pollyanna*, none of which either he or I saw with our eyes. Perhaps a church would have been better, but the darkness in a cinema seemed to calm the fears and the dreadful thoughts which penetrated one's own brains.

I saw Mervyn the next day, and his hand was still, his leg was still. His speech was impaired but this, I was told, was a normal reaction to such a shock.

*　　　*　　　*

It was my eldest son's twenty-first birthday within a week of the operation. I felt he must have his day, and so we had a party at home, with close friends and relations. Sebastian was saddened by his father's absence, and at the same time I was hoping that Mervyn would within weeks or months be able to resume a life which had been so rudely interrupted.

He was in the hospital for about two weeks, and on coming home he was noticeably calmer, with his physical disabilities greatly improved, and yet the speech was still slurred and his thoughts still slow and confused. It was a matter of time, we were told again, before his brain would clear, so delicate it is. I always think of the beginning of *Titus Alone* when I think of his brain, unique.

To North, South, East and West it was not long before his landmarks fled him.

It was not to be long before *his* landmarks fled him, but slowly and remorselessly. The signposts were becoming harder to read, the mist was descending, but with the frailty of a gauze curtain between the audience and the player.

*   *   *

He spent his days trying to recapture the felicity of drawing, but finding it more difficult, although his hand was steadier.

Many years ago, in Sark, he had written a long narrative poem called *The Rhyme of the Flying Bomb*, which had been written almost in one burst of writing, day and night.

This poem had been lost for years, but one day, on sorting all the multifarious papers in his cupboards, it appeared almost as suddenly as a ship in a fog.

There seemed to be little need for revision. It was sent out and accepted by Dent, who wished Mervyn to do drawings for it. When I thought of the enormous difficulty of his drawings for Balzac, I must say my heart sank, but the publishers were very anxious that he should produce not just a poem but drawings to complement the text.

It was unbelievable. The ease with which he had worked in the past, ideas growing upon ideas, cartoons for drawings being made, for all the books he had illustrated, not with ease, but with fluency and amplitude. And now, the brain could not grasp ideas long enough to hold them and turn them into visual life. Once again, I tried to work out where the illustrations (if that is what they were) should go, and I sat with him, until we were both exhausted, trying to make the salient picture. Seeing them in the book, I doubt if anyone could know the pain with which those drawings were imbued.

The book was published in 1962. There were very few reviews, and after a certain interval it took its place with the several other books which had been remaindered.

Two years later a radio programme made from it was broadcast on the Third Programme, with most evocative music by Tristram Carey, and touching performances by Marius Goring as the sailor, and Marjorie Westbury as the baby. This, strangely enough, had wonderful notices.

*   *   *

That was the last book, although I have tragic notes for the beginning of a fourth *Titus*—the gropings of a man, wishing to write something to surpass anything he had already done; a huge vision, and nothing to allow it to manifest itself.

There was an exhibition of his drawings in the Portobello Road, to which he went, and was still able to talk moderately coherently, but there were less and less times when he could meet people. If we went out, it was usually thought that he was drunk or drugged, and offence was often taken. I longed to shelter him, and I bear resentment of the intelligent ones who turned their backs on him, thinking he was insulting them. There is pain in seeing so gentle a man cold-shouldered.

Nothing was right or could be so ever again. And yet does one ever give up hoping? We went to yet another specialist, who diagnosed encephalitis, which often occurs with Parkinson's Disease. Too late, his opinion was that there should have been no operation, but how can anyone know? The implications were told to me, and we went home where the television was full-steam. The tears which were flooding my eyelids had to be stemmed until my daughter was in bed.

★   ★   ★

I do not wish to write further of an illness that left a man bereft in mind, but I wished to write this book for a man, unique and alone.

Rather than a little pain, I would be thief
To the organ-chords of grief
That toll through me
With a burial glory.

Wherefore my searching dust
If not to breathe the Gust
Of every quarter
Before I scatter,

And to divine
The lit or hooded Ghost, and take for mine
The double pulse; so come
Forth from your midnight tomb.

Cold grief
I would be thief
Of you,
Until my bones breed hemlock through and through.

'Hallo . . . Hallo . . . Are you there? Oh, are you there? Darling, are you there?'

The line was there . . . The possibilities of communication were there, but he was not there.

'Hallo . . . Hallo, I MUST go on saying it. I want to see you. I want to speak to you. I want you to answer me . . . I want life to be as it used to be. Darling, I'm wilting from the need of you.'

The silence remained, but the line which had been connected for thirty years was frail, and only a few unintelligible sounds could be heard. Despair gave way to the hope which always lay in my mind.

'Darling . . . I haven't seen you for twelve years. . . . Nearly a third of our life-time together. Answer me. . . . Say something, tell me.'

The silence remained. A crackling of sound. . . . Noises which were incomprehensible. Silence alone is better than incomprehension.

'Where are you? Where have you gone? I can see you, and I can touch you, but YOU have gone. I am coming to see you. Each time before I see you, I flower . . . Each time I have seen you, I die.'

Silence . . . Always the silence of a foreign language. Unbelievable that what had been rich, funny, vibrant, had become vacant.

'I am coming to see you. I long to. I have forgotten all now, but the past. The intense joy of it. The madness and the love. I will be with you today.'

There was no sound, but a series of sounds that I have heard but do not understand. Sounds from a world so far away. Is it an empty world . . . As desolate as I think it is, or is it peopled with visions? A world exclusive to you? Somewhere, may I share a little of that world?

The silence was now so white, . . . so untrammelled that speaking could do nothing but violate it.

There was a journey. There was fear that hope was unfounded. There were people. There was no silence. There was nothing, and there was hope clinging like a wet garment, so close to me.

The red buses . . . Strings of them . . . Not silent . . . Took me. There is the waiting and there is never silence. There are the black conductors, and the Cockney conductors, and the Irish conductors. Laughs sometimes, the lusty wit of the office cleaners. The pushing in the North End Road, the burdens of string bags full of cut-price detergents, vegetables, and sometimes even flowers, and I am making my way to you. . . . Full of hope, with sweets for you. I see you, my dark man, and my lover, full of aspiration. . . . Full of hope. I've forgotten about God. Once he was part of our universe, but he has gone, and the thin line has gone, and there is nothing left but what I know of you. Dark man . . . Funny man . . . Gentle man. Man that made life something new each day. Where are you? Please tell me where you have gone.

You said, 'Each day we live is a glass room.' It is, and it is so easily shattered. Every time when I see you, the glass is in one piece. Each time I leave you it is shattered.

Quickly, I want to see you. Slowly the door is unlocked. The niceties of life are fulfilled. 'Good morning,' to the white-coated man. 'How cold it is. What a lovely day. The crocuses are coming up.' The squirrels are darting jerkily across the drive. 'Good morning,' again. Pleasant people who do not know who they have in their possession, so lost and so alone are you.

I go down the cold stairs, and sometimes you have heard my voice, from above, as I say my platitudes. There is a

shuffling. I am afraid you are going to fall. I'm always afraid
for you. Sometimes there is no sound, and I open your door,
to your room, but no longer to you.

Quiet empty room. Quiet empty man. Your eyes look, and
do not see. Your ears hear, and do not hear. Your mouth
opens and closes and says nothing. Your hands hold a pencil,
and let it fall. Your feet move, but do not walk.

Then suddenly the eyes focus, and they smile. Your voice
speaks, and I understand, then it is all gone again. You try to
lift a chocolate from the table, and it falls.

I show you your books—that you have written, and which
are you, but you don't see them. I read to you the wise words
of the men who judge them, but those words fall upon stony
ground. You have gone away, and I can't find the way with
you.

I want the vision of you, as you were. Are you *you*? or have
you gone?

We sit silently, and then you are restless. You want to move
and cannot. You want to speak and cannot, and the silence no
longer has peace in it. The beautiful silence.

I give you a pencil, and I prop a sketch-book on your knee.
The pencil falls, and the book drops off your knee.

Sometimes, I make a feeble joke, which used to make our
children laugh when they were very small. You do and can
still laugh. 'Mary Rose sat on a pin. Mary Rose.'

A squirrel comes nervously in sharp little movements to
stand with its hands crossed outside your window. I throw
crumbs to it, and quick as a pickpocket they have disappeared,
before the pigeons or the sea-gulls or the sparrows have a
chance to battle for them.

Such small happenings now. So little to divert you. Now it
is time to go. When I leave you, I say 'Goodbye', but goodbye
was said many years ago, before we knew we were saying it.

And now you sit amongst others, who sit because they are

old. With their pasts known to themselves alone. Is it patience or tiredness which makes them so still? Are they empty of everything? Their eyes seem to be. Are their hearts too?

You look almost like them, and I want to say that you are not. But in the presence of such silent silence, I cannot think of you as any different from the other tired people.

You have gone. I long to see you again.

MERVYN PEAKE

A bibliography of his principal works

Captain Slaughterboard drops Anchor, London, Country Life, 1939

Ride a Cock-Horse and Other Nursery Rhymes, London, Chatto and Windus, 1940

Shapes and Sounds, London, Chatto and Windus, 1941

Rhymes without Reason, London, Eyre and Spottiswoode, 1944

Titus Groan, London, Eyre and Spottiswoode, 1946

Craft of the Lead Pencil, London, Wingate, 1946

Letters from a Lost Uncle from Polar Regions, London, Eyre and Spottiswoode, 1948

Drawings of Mervyn Peake, London, Grey Walls Press, 1949

The Glassblowers, London, Eyre and Spottiswoode, 1950

Gormenghast, London, Eyre and Spottiswoode, 1950

Mr Pye, London, Heinemann, 1953

Figures of Speech, London, Gollancz, 1954

Titus Alone, London, Eyre and Spottiswoode, 1959

The Rhyme of the Flying Bomb, London, Dent, 1962

Poems and Drawings, London, Keepsake Press, 1965

A Reverie of Bone, London, Rota, 1967

Other books illustrated by him

Carroll (L.): *Hunting of the Snark*, London, Chatto and Windus, 1941

Joad (C. E. M.): *Adventures of the Young Soldier*, London, Faber and Faber, 1943

Crisp (Q.): *All This and Bevin Too*, London, Nicholson and Watson, 1943

Coleridge (S. T.): *The Rime of the Ancient Mariner*, London, Chatto and Windus, 1943

Laing (A. M.): *Prayers and Graces*, London, Gollancz, 1944

Hole (C.): *Witchcraft in England*, London, Batsford, 1945

Grimm (J.) and (W. C.): *Household Tales*, London, Eyre and Spottiswoode, 1946

Collis (M. S.): *Quest for Sita*, London, Faber and Faber, 1946

Carroll (L.): *Alice's Adventures in Wonderland, etc.*, Stockholm, Zephyr, 1946

Stevenson (R. L.): *Dr Jekyll and Mr Hyde*, London, Folio Society, 1948

Stevenson (R. L.): *Treasure Island*, London, Eyre and Spottiswoode, 1949

Haynes (D. K.): *Thou Shalt Not Suffer a Witch*, London, Methuen, 1949

Wyss (J. D.): *The Swiss Family Robinson*, London, Heirloom Library, 1950

Drake (H. B.): *The Book of Lyonne*, London, Falcon, 1952

Palmer (E. C.): *The Young Blackbird*, London, Wingate, 1953

Austin (P. B.): *The Wonderful Life . . . of Tom Thumb* (2 vols.), Stockholm, Radio Sweden, 1954/55

Sander (A.): *Men: a Dialogue between Women*, London, Cresset, 1955

Drake (H. B.): *Oxford English Course for Secondary Schools, Book 1*, London, Oxford University Press, 1957

Laing (A. M.): *More Prayers and Graces*, London, Gollancz, 1957

Judah (A.): *The Pot of Gold and two other tales*, London, Faber and Faber, 1959

Balzac (H. de): *Droll Stories*, London, Folio Society, 1961

His Principal Exhibitions

Exhibited for first and last time at R.A.	April 1931 (aged 20)
Soho Group, Regal Restaurant—Soho	1931
The Twenties Group, Werthern Gallery	1932 and 1933
Sark Group at newly opened modern art gallery in Sark	1933
Sark Group, Cooling Galleries (London)	1934
R.B.A.	1935
Leger Galleries	1936
Calmann Gallery	1938
Leicester Galleries	1939
Satirical Drawings of our Time, Delius Giese Gallery	1939
Drawings sent to America during the war for exhibition	1942
Paintings of 'Glassblowers' exhibited at National Gallery during the war (now in Birmingham Art Gallery)	1943
Adams Gallery	1946
Arcade Gallery	1946
Waddington Galleries	approx. 1956
Collectors Gallery, Portobello Road	approx. 1957
Collectors Gallery, Portobello Road	approx. 1958
Upper Grosvenor Galleries	approx. 1967

Drawing from *The Hunting of the Snark* presented to the Queen for Prince Charles

Drawings in Private Collections in England, Ireland, Scotland and U.S.A.

Drawings in Victoria and Albert Museum

Painting in Imperial War Museum (of R.A.F. officers, commissioned by War Office)

Sets and costumes designed for *The Insect Play* by the Brothers Capek for the Little Theatre, 1936

Exhibition of diaries and manuscripts, Westminster City Public Library, 1968

Posthumous exhibition at his school, Eltham College, of diaries, paintings, manuscripts, etc., 1969

Exhibition at Swansea University, 1970

INDEX